FORWARD ▸ FACING™ TRAUMA THERAPY

FORWARD▸FACING™ TRAUMA THERAPY

Healing the Moral Wound

by Author

J. ERIC GENTRY, PhD

with Ilisa Keith Block

Published by

Compassion Unlimited

Sarasota, Florida

Forward-Facing™ Trauma Therapy: Healing the Moral Wound

Published by:
Compassion Unlimited
PO Box 15729
Sarasota, Florida 34277

Cover artwork by Bruce Rolff
Cover and book design by Michelle Radomski
Illustrations by Susan Tower

Printed in the United States of America
First Printing, 2016
ISBN: 978-0-9975292-0-3 (Paperback)
ISBN: 978-0-9975292-1-0 (E-book)

For further information and/or to purchase *Forward-Facing Trauma Therapy*, visit the author's websites at www.forward-facing.com or www.FFTTbook.com.

This book is dedicated to the many women and men
I have known who found the courage to overcome
their fear of change and take their first courageous steps
toward new lives filled with dignity, meaning and purpose.

"Your outer journey may contain a million steps;

your inner journey only has one:

the step you are taking right now."

— ECKHART TOLLE —

author of

The Power of Now: A Guide to Spiritual Enlightenment

Table of Contents

Acknowledgments

First and foremost, I wish to humbly and gratefully honor the thousands of trauma survivors who have trusted me to accompany them on their courageous journeys of healing and transcendence.

I am fortunate to stand on the shoulders of some of the giants of my field. Chief among them is Charles Figley, my dissertation chair and mentor. Thanks to his wisdom, support, and unflagging kindness, I was able to complete my doctoral program at a time when I was in danger of losing myself forever. My deepest thanks also go to two of my closest friends and colleagues: Anna Baranowsky, with whom I co-authored the book *Trauma Practice: Tools for Stabilization and Recovery*; and Robert Rhoton, director of the Arizona Trauma Institute, vice president of IATP, and one of the most gifted trauma clinicians I know. I must also acknowledge the profound debt of gratitude I owe to Joe M, my first and current sponsor, who has saved my life and soul more times than I can count, and my therapist Charlie Yeargan, who shepherded me through the painful process of confronting and resolving my traumatic past.

Additionally, I would like to thank Mike Dubi, president of IATP; Mason and his family; Jim Dietz, Jacque Gentry, my sponsees, and the Fellowship for your contributions to this work and my life.

Most of all, I owe this book and my wonderful life to Marjie, my wise and lovely partner whose grace and integrity serve as a living testament to the principles of this book.

Introduction

"When we are no longer able to change a situation, we are challenged to change ourselves."

— VIKTOR E. FRANKL —

Shortly before I began writing this book, I found myself thinking about the opening lines to *A Tale of Two Cities*, the historical novel by Charles Dickens, and how apt they seem to our lives today.

> *"It was the best of times, it was the worst of times, it was the age of wisdom, it was the age of foolishness, it was the epoch of belief, it was the epoch of incredulity, it was the season of Light, it was the season of Darkness, it was the spring of hope, it was the winter of despair…"*

By all meaningful measures,[1] Americans are living through the safest and least violent period in human history. Nevertheless, far too many of us are enduring lives of quiet—and sometimes not so quiet—desperation. We feel overwhelmed by stress, riddled with anxiety, felled by depression, and trapped in patterns of self-destructive behavior we believe we are powerless to change. Yet positive change is not only possible, it's inevitable when you learn and apply the skills I'll be describing in the pages to come.

This book is a message of hope, a bridge from despair to optimal living. Whether your stress level is relatively mild or you're among the 8 million adults[2] contending each year with full-blown posttraumatic stress disorder (PTSD), you *can* eliminate stress and its destructive aftereffects from your life. You *can* become your best self, someone worthy of respect and admiration. You *can* overcome the seemingly insurmountable obstacles standing between you and a meaningful and satisfying life. And you can achieve all of this by using methods that are simple, straightforward, and entirely under your control.

You and I will take a journey together from hardship to healing. We'll begin by exploring some of the common myths and misconceptions about the causes and meaning of stress. We'll examine the destruction it can wreak on our bodies, our minds, our spirits, and our relationships. We'll discover the triggers that can lead us to act reflexively in ways that we deeply regret afterwards. Then, we'll learn how to gently move out of this reflexive reactivity. Most importantly, we'll consider what it means to live an intentional life and how cultivating the skill of interoception, or "bodifulness," can help us achieve this essential goal. Along the way, I'll share some inspiring stories about women and men I've known who successfully put these lessons into practice, vanquishing stress, regaining their resilience, and finding new joy, optimization, and fulfillment in their lives.

Why I Wrote This Book

I began my own journey in 1982, when I started working as a nighttime houseparent at an adolescent crisis shelter in Huntington, West Virginia. Over the next several years, I waged a losing battle with depression and addiction. Twice, I failed to complete my undergraduate training. Finally, in 1988, I surrendered this fight and began a 12-step recovery program. Soon afterwards, I returned to school and discovered, to my surprise, that I was a good student. I earned high marks and was able to successfully complete my bachelor's and master's degrees, Certificate of Advanced Study, and finally, my doctorate in 2007.

During the difficult years I spent working with troubled adolescents, I learned something crucial that would shape my subsequent career as a clinician, researcher, academician, consultant, and professional speaker. I became convinced that the violent and destructive behaviors my teenage clients displayed were rooted in traumatic experiences they had endured as children. In professional terms, they were suffering not from some form of psychopathology but from the effects of overly adaptive defenses and strategies they had acquired early on to survive and cope with chronic abuse and neglect.

However, my most important breakthroughs in understanding the destructive effects of traumatic stress came from working through my own painful traumatic history. In 1991, after two years of recovery, I suddenly began to experience intense and overwhelming PTSD symptoms. I was unable to concentrate on my work and found myself indulging in increasingly risky, self-destructive behaviors. My relationships began to suffer, and eventually, I reached the point of being overcome by terror at the mere prospect of leaving my house. I knew I had to do *something* to save myself but felt powerless to do it on my own. So I sought out the help of a professionally trained therapist.

Working with my therapist, I came to understand that all my symptoms—my addiction, reckless risk taking, depression, self-loathing, and suicidal thoughts—were not character defects or signs of pathology, but rather sophisticated coping strategies I had developed to survive the ongoing trauma I had experienced since early childhood. While this insight was both comforting and helpful, it was only a starting point. If I wanted to heal, I was told, I would have to confront my past and face down my traumatic memories.

This process proved to be so terrifying and overwhelming for me that I fled therapy. To this day, I don't know whether to attribute my subsequent relapse into chemical dependency to the brutal process of reliving my traumatic memories or to my resistance to fully investing in the process of recovery. Regardless, it was both a major setback and a hint of something positive to come.

In 1995, I returned to therapy and finished working through my traumatic past. I'm proud to say that I've been abstinent from all mind/mood-altering chemicals since that time. In 1996, I completed a year-long fellowship in psychotraumatology at the School of Medicine at West Virginia University. There, I studied under Dr. Louis Tinnin, a towering figure in the field of trauma research and treatment who has been described as "the greatest trauma mind of the 20th century."[3]

Lou taught me how to surgically resolve trauma memories using his hypnotic "Anamnesis" approach. After completing my fellowship, I spent six months thru-hiking the Appalachian Trail southbound from Mt. Katahdin in Maine to Springer Mountain in Georgia, a trek of some 2,168 miles. Renewed in body and spirit, I began my doctoral program in marriage and family therapy at Florida State University, where I focused primarily on trauma research and treatment.

At FSU, I was privileged to work with Professor Charles Figley, PhD—one of the pioneers and leading lights in the field of trauma research and treatment. In 1997, Charles and I jointly founded the Traumatology Institute and subsequently won that year's "Curriculum of the Year" award from the United Continuing Education Association. During the ensuing years, I trained thousands of clinicians in the science and treatment of traumatic stress, first at the Institute, then at the International Traumatology Institute, and currently, at the International Association of Trauma Professionals, where I serve as vice president.

During this period, I earned certifications in a veritable alphabet soup of treatment methodologies, including Dialectical Behavioral Therapy (DBT), Cognitive-Behavioral Therapy (CBT), Eye Movement Desensitization and Reprocessing (EMDR), and many more. In retrospect, however, I still consider the 12-step recovery program I entered in 1988 and the personal trauma therapy I began in 1991 to be the twin pillars on which I've built my career.

Since launching my clinical practice in 1990, I've had the privilege of walking with thousands of patients as they've confronted their pasts and healed their hurts. Along the way, my colleagues and I have developed a set of principles and techniques for eliminating stress and resolving trauma that have transformed my own life in ways that are far-reaching and profoundly positive. Now, I'm honored to share them with you. I hope you'll accept them in this spirit and begin your own journey of healing and transformation.

A Brief History of Trauma Therapy

We've learned a great deal about the treatment of traumatic stress since 1980, when the American Psychological Association first identified posttraumatic stress disorder as a diagnostic category in the third edition of the *Diagnostic and Statistical Manual of Mental Disorders* (DSM-III). Back then, the dominant treatment modality was "Implosion Therapy," which drew heavily on the concepts of "flooding" and "catharsis."

As the name implies, flooding consisted of guiding a trauma survivor through an arduous process of repeatedly describing and reliving the most painful aspects of their traumas until their repressed memories broke through their defenses and spilled into consciousness. When this occurred, the patient would "implode" and experience catharsis, a huge release of pent-up psychic energy and unprocessed pain. Only by reliving the traumatic experience and achieving this catharsis, it was believed, could the patient create a meaningful narrative that would purge the trauma of its intrusive power and destructive influence. This process, whether it was attained through hypnosis, suggestion, or simple recollection, was referred to as "abreaction."

Over time, the implosive model evolved into a form of cognitive behavioral therapy known as Prolonged Exposure Therapy (PE). Today, there is considerable research supporting the effectiveness of PE. In fact, it's now recognized as an evidence-based treatment for PTSD by the Department of Veterans Affairs.[4] However, the draconian process of flooding and implosion that forms the backbone of PE has proven to be so painful for many patients that as many as 30% drop out of treatment, according to some studies.[5]

In the 1990s, our understanding of PTSD advanced rapidly. This was driven, in part, by the influx of troubled combat personnel returning from extended tours of duty in Iraq and Afghanistan. According to the National Center for PTSD, "About 11–20 out of every 100 veterans (or between 11–20%) who served in Operations Iraqi Freedom (OIF) and Enduring Freedom (OEF) have PTSD in a given year." During that same period, "…about 12 out of every 100 Gulf War (Operation Desert Storm) veterans (or 12%) have PTSD."[6]

Another factor was the exciting research beginning to emerge from the relatively new discipline of brain science, which was offering compelling insights into the functioning of the brain and how this relates to cognition and memory formation, the development of psychopathology, the emergence of consciousness, and much more.

But in my view, the greatest gains in trauma treatment were fueled by two groundbreaking publications that appeared in 1992. The first was a paper co-written by psychologist Onno van der Hart, PhD, and psychiatrist Paul Brown entitled, "Abreaction Reevaluated," which was published in the journal, *Dissociation.* In this provocative article, the authors applauded the "innovative and effective" new methods being developed to treat traumatic memories and railed against "the persisting use of the controversial and, in the authors' view, outmoded concepts of abreaction and repression…"[7] Instead, van der Hart and Brown urged therapists to pursue a more compassionate treatment model in which survivors could shape and share narratives of their traumatic experiences while remaining physically relaxed, through techniques such as hypnosis.

That same year, psychiatrist Judith Lewis Herman published her seminal book, *Trauma and Recovery*, which proposed a three-phase approach to trauma treatment that contrasted sharply with the blunt force brutality of the abreaction model. In the first phase, the therapist focuses on establishing a trusting therapeutic relationship and constructing a foundation of stability and safety by teaching the client relaxation exercises, and, if necessary, prescribing medications. The actual trauma work begins in the next phase, remembrance and mourning, in which the therapist gently elicits the client's traumatic memories while helping them create a coherent narrative within the secure foundation established in phase one. In the final stage, reconnection and reintegration, the client learns to reconcile with their past, identify and repudiate aspects of their identity that have been imposed by their trauma, and find new richness and meaning in their lives.

Over the past two decades, a variety of treatment approaches have emerged that combine narrative with relaxation to help trauma survivors resolve their symptoms with minimal distress, including Eye Movement Desensitization and Reprocessing, Louis Tinnin's Anamnesis method, Visual-Kinesthetic Dissociation Technique, and Traumatic Incident Reduction. Other increasingly mainstream and widely used therapies include Cognitive Behavioral Therapy, Cognitive Processing Therapy, and such mindfulness-based approaches as Acceptance and Commitment Therapy.

This brings us to the present day, where we're poised to make a new evolutionary leap in the understanding and treatment of posttraumatic stress. Forward-Facing Trauma

Therapy (FFTT) is a gentle, self-directed, real-time treatment method that doesn't require survivors to painfully excavate—and then wallow in—their most painful memories. Instead, they learn simple, intuitive techniques that allow them to control how their brains and bodies react *while* they are being triggered and re-experiencing the intrusive feelings, images, and thoughts that are often evoked by severe stress or trauma. In the chapters to come, we'll explore the three-pronged FFTT methodology and explain how and why the techniques work so effectively. We'll examine the underlying biology and explain how anyone experiencing stress can apply FFTT to achieve constructive change and an enduring sense of joy, self-worth, and personal integrity.

FFTT is not a panacea. It cannot inoculate you against sadness or shield you from the shocks and losses we all experience from time to time. But it *can* help you become the person you *choose* to be, someone who faces life feeling lighter, stronger, wiser, and more hopeful. It *can* provide you with the tools you need to build better relationships with your loved ones and live an intentional, principled life. When you encounter setbacks, you'll be able to take them in stride and rebound with fresh reserves of energy and confidence. You'll be able to reach beyond your comfort zone and take worthwhile risks that challenge you and help you achieve the growth and maturation that are our human birthright. And you will be able to do all of this within a relaxed and comfortable body!

When stress no longer rules you, you'll be able to perform at your best, both at work and at play. In Dickens' words, you'll emerge from darkness into light, from despair into hope, from foolishness into wisdom, and from incredulity into faith.

Now, let the journey begin.

CHAPTER 1

The Myth of Stress

> *"Change the way you look at things and the things you look at change."*
>
> — WAYNE W. DYER —

You're stuck in traffic on your way to work, knowing that you're going to be late once again when the driver on your left suddenly cuts in front of you without warning. You feel a jolt of fear and slam on the brakes, missing his rear bumper by scant inches. He doesn't even look back or raise a hand in apology. He just drives on, oblivious and unconcerned. That's when you snap.

You veer out into traffic and pull up alongside him, rolling down your passenger-side window and screaming insults. He responds by pulling down *his* window and making an obscene gesture as he revs his engine and races past you. You become even more enraged and briefly consider smashing your car into his. You'd love to teach him a lesson he'll never forget. That's when you notice the little boy and girl cowering in the back seat of his car; eyes wide, staring at you in obvious terror. With shaking hands, you roll up your window and fight for control. You're still angry, but now you also feel deeply ashamed.

This is a betrayal of your best self and your commitment to a principled life. It's not who you are or how you want to live. It's not you at all. Or is it?

You and I are among the most fortunate humans ever to inhabit this beautiful green planet. Those of us who live in first world nations are doubly blessed to reside in regions where even our most disadvantaged citizens enjoy a standard of living that would have seemed inconceivable to those living just a few generations ago. Why then do so many of us take such little pleasure in our lives? Why do we feel so tense and trapped that we sometimes find ourselves striking out against others, often at the people we care most deeply about? In short, why are we so stressed out? And what exactly *is* stress anyway?

In part, the answer is shrouded in the mists of our evolutionary heritage. It dates back to a time when humans—like every other animal—faced very real threats to our survival. Lacking imposing claws, fangs, poisons, or armored skin, humans were ill-equipped to deter attacks from the dangerous predators we encountered on the African savannah. Our survival depended on the speed with which we could accurately perceive these threats and respond by fighting or fleeing.

Over the ensuing millennia, our bodies and brains evolved to optimize this process, enabling us to quickly and efficiently release a potent cocktail of chemicals and compounds that activated our muscles, sharpened our senses, and supercharged our metabolisms. This gave rise to a fight-or-flight response that is still operating at peak efficiency within the deepest recesses of our primitive brains. This acute stress response mobilizes our bodies into action by triggering increases in our heart rate and breathing, constricting our blood vessels, and tightening our muscles. It gives us the rapid boost of energy we once needed to escape the hungry lion poised to attack us.

Figure 1: The Threat-Response System

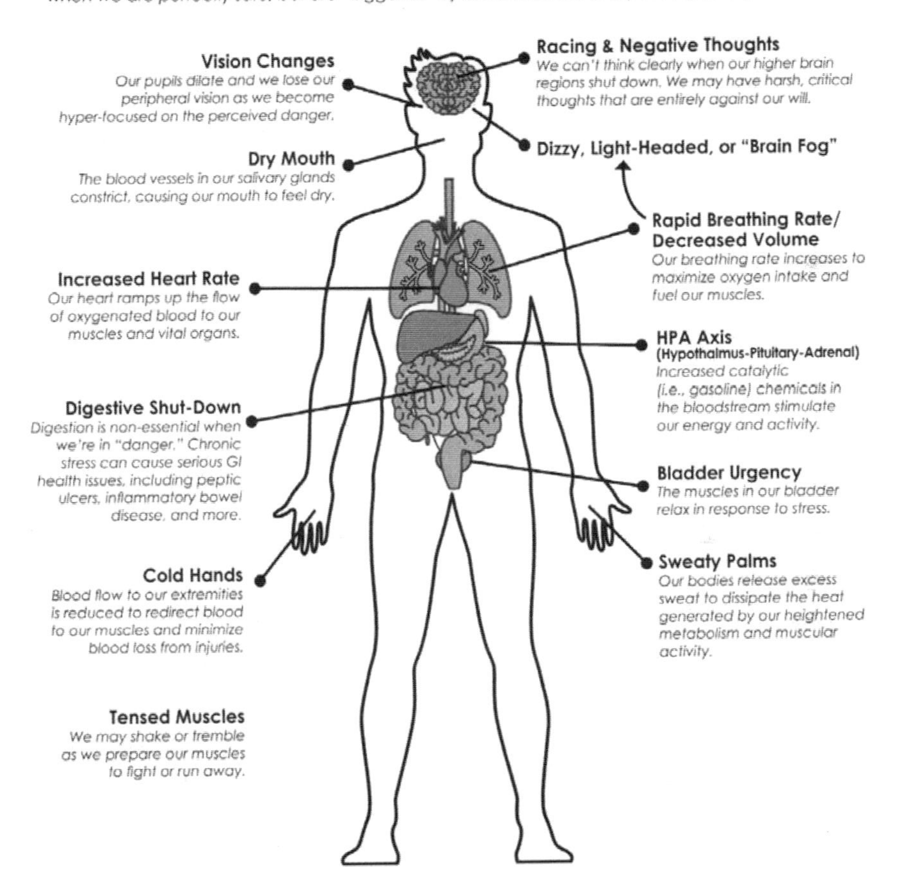

In the modern world, of course, very few of us encounter lions on our way to work. However, the primitive reactive part of our brain that responds to imminent danger cannot distinguish between a physical threat like a lion attack and the more abstract threats we commonly encounter in our daily lives. When our boss yells at us for missing a deadline or another driver cuts us off in traffic, our primitive reactive brains still propel us into a full-fledged fight-or-flight response as if our very lives were at stake.

Simply put, then, *stress is nothing more than a reaction to a perceived threat.* And, since it evolved in a very different environment than we live in today, our threat detection and response system is poorly attuned to the realities of modern life. All too often, a small irritation or disappointment plunges us into full-blown reactivity as if our very lives were at stake. Fortunately, we can learn to attenuate this response and apply the appropriate amount of energy and action to the challenges we encounter in our daily lives.

For those of us struggling with stress, this realization can be profoundly empowering. It means that stress is not an externally imposed feature of our environment that we are powerless to control. Quite the contrary, stress is an automatic response to perceived danger that exists entirely within our own bodies and minds. Once we learn how to control this response, we can eliminate our entrenched reactivity and eradicate stress from our lives.

This insight struck home for me with particular poignancy one evening in late September 2001 as I was doing some online research at my hotel in lower Manhattan. Outside my window, search and rescue teams were sifting through the wreckage and rubble that were all that remained of the Twin Towers. The words on the website almost leapt off the screen: "Disease is the absence of effective antibodies, not the presence of a toxic environment." This simple statement affected me deeply. In that moment, my perspectives on disease and trauma started to crystallize in a new way. I began to turn my focus from the grief and horror that so many of us felt following the tragedy of the 9/11 attacks. Instead, I resolved to help our nation and its citizens repair, rebuild, and develop the "antibodies" we would need to resist the toxic effects of terrorism and to recover our faith and hopes for the future.

In the days and weeks that followed, I came to recognize that stress is best understood as the absence of effective coping strategies (i.e., "antibodies"), rather than the presence of a threatening (i.e., "toxic") environment. This insight had profound implications. As a therapist, my primary goal would be to help clients acquire a robust immunity to stress by controlling themselves rather than their surroundings. This meant helping my clients shift from an external locus of control, in which they felt overwhelmed and victimized, to an internal locus of control, in which they developed the resilience and sense of self-efficacy they would need to survive and flourish as they moved forward in their lives. This paradigm shift in perspective has become one of the cornerstones of my work for the past fifteen years.

The Stress Continuum

Our threat-response system plays another essential role, too. It provides the energy and strength we need to successfully pursue meaningful goals and experience joy, anticipation, and ecstasy in our lives. A short bout of mild stress can sometimes be highly beneficial, sharpening our concentration, helping us learn, and preparing our muscles for quick and decisive action. A star baseball player, for example, would be hard-pressed to hit a fastball traveling at 100 miles per hour if he were utterly unconcerned about maintaining his place on the starting lineup.

Likewise, a student preparing for an important test would have little motivation to study hard if she simply didn't care about her grades.

The relationship between optimal performance and the physical and mental arousal induced by stress was first identified by American psychologists Robert Mearns Yerkes and John Dillingham Dodson back in 1908. Contemporary psychologists have since refined these insights and codified them in the Yerkes-Dodson Law. As shown below, low levels of arousal are necessary for good performance. No one runs quickly, plays blistering guitar solos, or successfully negotiates multi-million-dollar deals while they are napping. However, once the energy in our bodies climbs beyond optimal levels, our performance drops precipitously. This occurs sooner when we are engaged in complex and challenging tasks, especially those that are mentally demanding.

Figure 2: Yerkes-Dodson Law

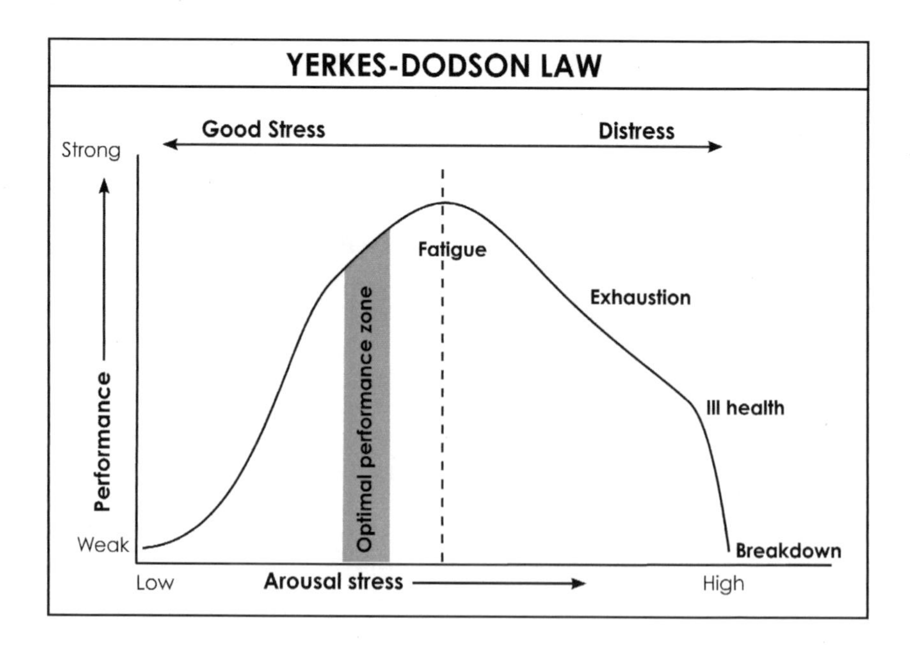

However, this kind of mild, transient stress is very different from the severe and prolonged stress that can be so devastating to our bodies and minds. Chronic stress has been linked to serious health issues ranging from severe depression and cognitive impairment to increased risk of cardiovascular disease and autoimmune disorders. And the impact of chronic stress can quickly rise to traumatic proportions when it's associated in our primitive brains with past experiences we found to be particularly painful or frightening. The deleterious effects of this painful past learning are further heightened if we are socially isolated or lack emotional support from someone important to us.

Figure 3: Symptoms of Stress

SYMPTOMS OF STRESS

Physical	Emotional & Cognitive	Behavioral	Spiritual & Relational
• Fatigue • Irritability • GI Distress • Headaches • Tension • Dis-ease • Weakened Immune System • Pain	• Anxiety • Depression • Difficulty Concentrating • Anger • Sadness • Pessimism/ Cynicism • Judgmental of Self/Others • Forgetfulness • Self-Destructiveness	• Aggression • Avoidance • Overeating • Alcohol/ Drug Use • Isolation • Perfectionism • Sarcasm • Excessive Risk-Taking • Volatility	• Hopelessness • Disconnection • Self-Loathing • Guilt & Shame • Lack of Joy • Fearfulness • Loss of Meaning & Purpose • Greed

The American Psychological Association defines trauma as "an emotional response to a terrible event like an accident, rape, or natural disaster."[8] Traumas like these can wreak havoc on our personal sense of safety and well-being, causing symptoms ranging from extreme irritability and depression to all-out flashbacks and night terrors. But we may also have a traumatic stress response to situations in which there is no present danger. This can occur whenever a painful or traumatic experience from our past intrudes into our perceptual systems. Any painful past experience, no matter how brief or seemingly innocuous, can erupt into our consciousness, causing us to perceive a threat where none exists. In my practice, we conceive of trauma as arising from three different types of painful learning that may occur singly or in combination.

Primary Trauma

Primary trauma occurs when we directly experience one or more events that threaten our well-being and over which we have little or no control. Consider the case of "Jill," a 38-year-old stay-at-home mom of two little boys, "Allen" (7) and "Aaron" (5). Throughout her childhood, Jill endured severe abuse and neglect. Both of her parents were alcoholics. When she was 10, her parents divorced. Soon afterwards, her father abandoned the family entirely, leaving Jill in the sole care of her mother, who became increasingly physically and verbally abusive throughout Jill's teen years.

School became Jill's only refuge from the fear and darkness of her home. But because she was so ashamed of herself and her family, Jill made very few friends there. "I never knew what

I was coming home to after school," she explained. So she tried her best to be invisible at home and with her peers. "It seems like, growing up, any time I got noticed, I got hurt."

Jill's life improved dramatically at age 17, when she was accepted at a local junior college and moved into student housing. She went on to earn her associate's degree and subsequently pursued a successful career in real estate. However, her relationships were another matter entirely.

In her 20s, Jill dated a number of eligible men. But, whenever a relationship appeared to be heading toward commitment or marriage, she would become frightened and end it. After several of these failed relationships, Jill finally entered therapy at age 28. There, she discovered how her abusive childhood had contaminated her perception of loving relationships. Her primitive reactive mind had learned to associate intimacy with abuse and did its best to protect her by flooding her body and conscious mind with an overpowering urge to flee.

Childhood traumas like Jill's can have devastating lifelong effects. This has been demonstrated conclusively in the Adverse Childhood Experiences (ACE) Study conducted by the Centers for Disease Control and Prevention (CDC) in collaboration with Kaiser Permanente's Health Appraisal Clinic in San Diego. As noted on the CDC website, "...certain experiences are major risk factors for the leading causes of illness and death as well as poor quality of life in the United States. It is critical to understand how some of the worst health and social problems in our nation can arise as a consequence of adverse childhood experiences."[9]

Secondary Trauma

We don't have to personally experience traumatic events to become traumatized. A child can become traumatized by seeing her father beating her mother. A soldier can become traumatized by seeing a fellow solider severely injured or killed in combat. Any of us can witness traumatic events through the media or our work, or by serving as a caregiver for a loved one contending with a serious illness. This kind of secondary trauma can creep up on us slowly and insidiously through a series of small but ongoing shocks. Consider the case of my patient "Mark," a successful physician at a Midwest hospital.

In our first session, Mark walked into my office with downcast eyes and a shambling gait. Over the course of the next hour, he shared the desperation and despair he felt about virtually every aspect of his life. He described how his marriage of 30 years had devolved into a "business partnership" devoid of caring and intimacy. He and his wife slept in separate bedrooms, kept separate schedules, and spent as little time as possible in each other's company.

Professionally, Mark was at a standstill. He no longer took any pleasure or pride in his practice. He felt overstressed by his daily routine and bereft of the excitement and desire to help others that had first attracted him to medicine as a young man. Now, at 58, he was seriously considering abandoning medicine entirely, saying, "I'm afraid my job is going to kill me."

Over the past 18 months, Mark had gained 30 pounds. "I know I need to eat healthy and exercise," he acknowledged. "But after working a shift, I just can't seem to find the energy to get to the gym." His alcohol consumption had also increased, in part to help numb his continual distress and in part to combat the chronic insomnia that was robbing him of restful sleep. One day, Mark turned to me, with tears in his eyes, and asked, "How did it get this bad? I don't care about anything anymore. I just want to be done."

Mark's trauma had taken decades to reach such crisis proportions. Although he strove to retain his professional detachment, his constant exposure to illness and death over the years had gradually and insidiously taken its toll. From the standpoint of the most primitive part of his mind, the illness and death he witnessed were direct threats to his own health and safety. In small, unconscious, incremental steps, Mark became overwhelmed by trauma until it undermined his health, his marriage, and his career.

Environmental Trauma

As unlikely as it may seem, we don't even have to experience or witness trauma to become traumatized ourselves. Trauma is like an infection. If you're exposed long enough to someone who has been traumatized, you may become traumatized yourself. What's more, trauma like this can be passed down from one generation to the next through changes to our genomes that affect our stress-response systems and the threshold and intensity of our fight-or-flight responses.

Since World War II, for example, a variety of research studies have suggested that children of Holocaust survivors are especially vulnerable to the effects of stress and more likely to experience symptoms of posttraumatic stress disorder.[10] Although they never experienced the horrors their parents endured in the death camps, these offspring may still face increased risks of obesity, hypertension, insulin resistance, and other age-related metabolic syndromes.

"Joshua," a 24-year-old African-American man living in New York City, is an example of someone who was affected by environmental stress. On the surface, Joshua's childhood was a calm and happy one. As an only child with a large extended family, he was showered with love and attention from his parents, aunts, uncles, and cousins. Although his father, "Albert," had little education and few marketable skills, he managed to earn a steady income and support the family as a bus driver. And yet, Albert was not a happy man. He felt great bitterness about the poverty and racism he had endured as a child growing up in a small rural town in the 1950s. He filled his son's ears with stories about racial violence and warned Joshua never to trust white people, especially those in authority. He also pressured Joshua to do well in school so "you can make something of yourself."

Joshua was a quiet and compliant little boy. He studied hard and excelled at school, eventually earning a scholarship that enabled him to attend a prestigious university. At age 22, he graduated with a BA in finance. Although his parents urged him to attend graduate school, Joshua was eager to gain some practical business experience before continuing his education. When a large publishing firm offered him a sales position, he jumped at it.

Joshua's first year with the company was stellar. He made President's Club, where he caught the eye of several members of the senior management team. These included "John," the divisional vice president of marketing and sales. John was so impressed, he took Joshua under his wing and became his mentor. Joshua's career at the company appeared to be assured.

So it made little sense when Joshua reacted with utter panic after being asked by his sales manager to stop by his office to discuss something "important." "I thought he was going to fire me," Joshua explained. Instead, he was offered a promotion. He would now be leading his own sales team, with a great deal more responsibility and a significant bump in pay.

By all measures, Joshua should have been delighted. Instead, he became increasingly miserable. He found himself unable to sleep more than a few hours each night and started losing weight because he kept "forgetting" to eat. When I first met him, Joshua was deeply depressed and in such distress that he was harboring thoughts of suicide. Although he continued to excel at work, he was convinced he was about to be fired. "I cannot fail," he told me.

Working together, Joshua and I traced his distress to the trauma his father had endured during his youth. Gradually, Joshua came to understand how powerfully his father's rage and bitterness had affected him. Unconsciously, he deeply distrusted his manager and mentor, both of whom were white men. At any moment, he feared, they might turn on him just as other white men had turned on Albert. For Joshua, every promotion was a perceived threat. Every kind word was a potential preamble to the kind of abuse his father had suffered.

The Journey to Hope

Whatever the cause, when people like Mark, Jill, and Joshua experience traumatic stress, they become prisoners of their primitive reactive brains. They can no longer see their problems in perspective or apply their intelligence to find solutions. They perceive situations that others might find only mildly stressful as imminent threats to their survival. They torpedo relationships that might have provided the love, intimacy, and emotional support they so desperately need to heal. They face a higher risk of becoming addicted to alcohol, drugs, food, gambling, and other self-destructive behaviors in their frantic attempts to numb their pain. They may become especially vulnerable to the damaging effects of aging and disease. And, in the most tragic cases, they may lose their battle with stress and decide to take their own lives.

Yet, as we have seen, stress is not an elemental force of nature that exists outside of ourselves. It is not a black hole of loss and despair that we are powerless to escape. Instead, it is a flawed but still useful biological response to perceived threat that evolved over the millennia in a very different time and place than we live in today. It can be empowering and performance-enhancing or destructive and deadly. We can learn to control it and use it to our advantage, or we can let it control us and become its victim.

But first, we must clearly understand the biological imperatives that reside deep within our primitive brains and how they orchestrate the cascades and flows of the stress response. These physiological forces operate well below our consciousness, but once we learn how they're activated and set in motion, we can begin to gain mastery of the arousal, anxiety, and stress they cause us. At that point, we can embark on our journey to living fulfilling, intentional, and principle-based lives.

CHAPTER 2

How Stress Affects Our Minds and Bodies

"Between stimulus and response there is a space.
In that space is our power to choose our response.
In our response lies our growth and our freedom."

— VIKTOR E. FRANKL —

The human brain and nervous systems are marvels of engineering, with billions of cells interacting seamlessly to manage our bodies, interpret signals from our senses, and endow us with consciousness, reasoning, and spirituality. When it comes to perceiving and responding to threats, however, it's the most primitive parts of our brain and nervous system that often reign supreme.

The Traditional View

Until recently, we viewed the human threat-response system as consisting of two interacting neural networks that play complementary and opposing roles. These are the sympathetic nervous system and the parasympathetic nervous system.

Our Fight-or-Flight System

The sympathetic nervous system (SNS) is a bi-directional neural pathway that stretches from the spinal cord to virtually every major organ system, including the heart, lungs, liver, stomach, intestines, reproductive organs, and more. One of the SNS's chief responsibilities is to activate these organs into a heightened state of readiness—the fight-or-flight response—whenever we perceive a threat to our safety and survival. This threat detection process occurs extremely quickly and almost entirely below our conscious awareness.

Figure 4: The Sympathetic Nervous System

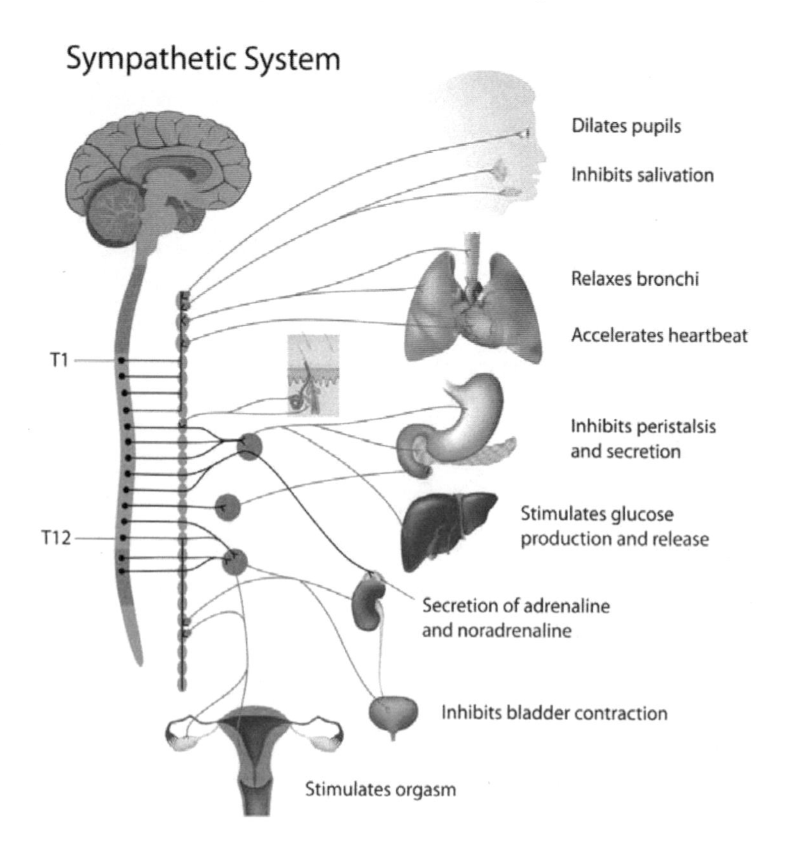

The fight-or-flight response begins in the brain's temporal lobe, which performs a variety of functions. These include prioritizing and deriving meaning from the flood of electrical signals arriving from our sense organs. Buried deep within the temporal lobe is the amygdala, a structure that helps us form and store long-term memories associated with emotional events. It is here that emotional learning first takes place and where previous learning can influence our perception of present danger.

Say, for example, you're among a group of early humans making your way across the African savannah. Suddenly, you hear the roar of an angry lion streaking toward you with claws extended and fangs bared. Before you can react, the lion seizes the man standing next to you and kills him as you watch, terrified and helpless to intervene. Your amygdala responds by creating and storing a powerful memory that includes all of the intense emotions you're feeling along with the sights, sounds, smells, and physical sensations you experienced during the lion attack. In the future, whenever you hear, see, smell, or feel something similar, your amygdala is likely to sound the alarm, causing the SNS to invoke the cascade of nerve signaling and hormonal secretions that collectively comprise the fight-or-flight response.

When this happens, our brains and bodies undergo dramatic changes designed to optimize our capabilities for strength and speed. Our heart rate and blood pressure spike as sugars and fats pour into our bloodstream to furnish us with a burst of energy. Blood is diverted away from our skin surface to our muscles, and our clotting function is accelerated to reduce the possibility of blood loss due to injury. Our muscle tension increases to prepare us for maximum sustained effort. Our immune system mobilizes to fight off infection in case our skin surface is punctured or damaged. We also become hypervigilant, with every sense straining to detect the source of the threat and determine our best options for fighting or fleeing.

This short-term mobilization has its costs, however. When the SNS is activated, it suppresses the higher centers of our brains—including the cerebral cortex—that enable us to reason, analyze, and make voluntary choices based on judgment and prior experience. Our visual acuity, impulse control, and fine motor control are degraded too, along with our ability to process and communicate complex thoughts. As a result, when the SNS is in control, our ability to calmly and accurately assess a threat goes out the window and we behave in ways that are reflexive, unthinking, and desperate.

These physiological responses may have been less problematic for ancient humans, whose decision-making options were mostly limited to fighting or fleeing. In the modern world, however, the situation is quite different. The kinds of threats we commonly encounter today are much more complex and abstract. We need full access to our reasoning and communication capabilities to respond effectively.

Our Feed and Breed System

Once the immediate danger has passed, a second system comes into play. Like the SNS, the parasympathetic nervous system (PNS) is a bi-directional neural pathway that runs between our spinal cord and our major organ systems. The PNS plays an opposing role to that of the SNS, calming our bodies and conserving our energy resources for more routine processes,

Figure 5: The Parasympathetic Nervous System

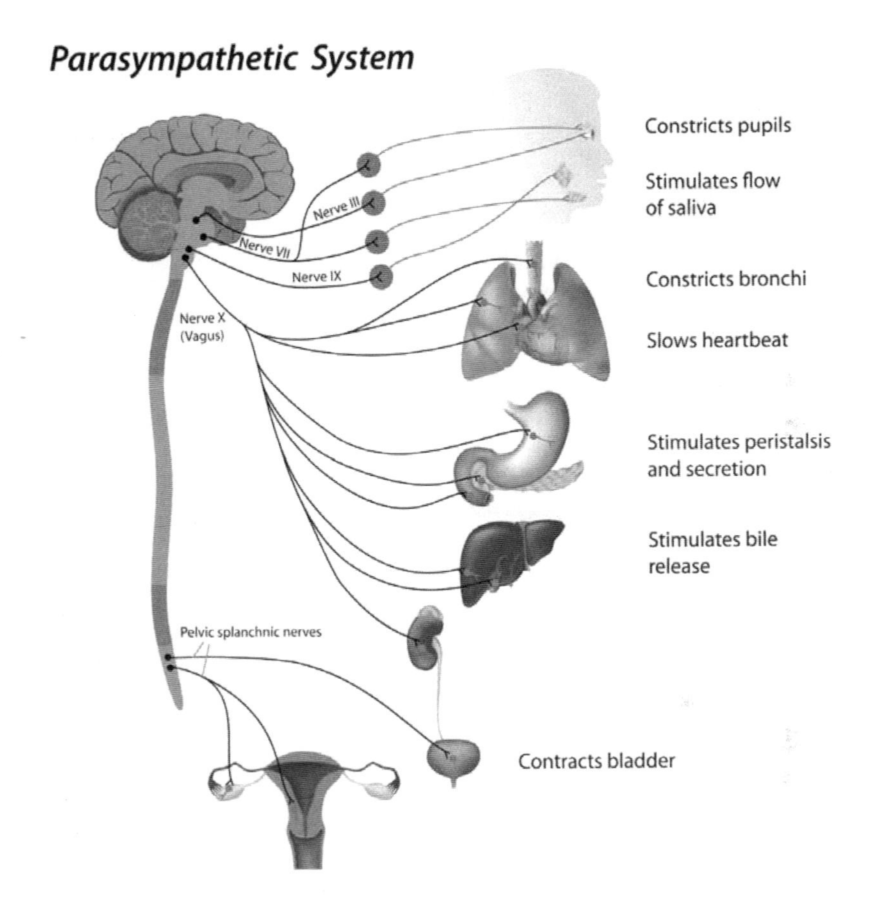

such as digestion and reproduction. For this reason, the PNS is sometimes referred to the "feed and breed" system.

With the parasympathetic nervous system at the controls, our heart rate slows back down, our muscles relax, and our blood pressure, blood chemistry, and immune systems return to normal. Our higher brain centers also come back online, restoring our abilities to think, assess, interact with others, and behave in accordance with our values and aspirations.

Ideally, this hand-off from the SNS to the PNS occurs efficiently, smoothly returning our bodies and brains to their pre-threat conditions. This process of regaining physical and mental equilibrium between the SNS and PNS is referred to as "homeostasis" and remains one of the primary goals of trauma therapy.

What We Know Now

Today, we have a much more nuanced understanding of our threat detection and response systems and how they influence behavior, thanks to the research and writings of renowned neuroscientist Dr. Stephen Porges, a pioneer in the field of biological psychology. His Polyvagal Theory dispenses with the older model of two systems—the SNS and PNS—that complement and oppose each other to achieve homeostasis. Instead, we now have three systems derived from splitting the PNS into two evolutionarily and operationally distinct subsystems: the dorsal vagal and the ventral vagal. Each of these subsystems is associated with a branch of the vagus nerve and a particular reaction to a perceived threat.

Our Passive Defense System

The dorsal vagal (DV) subsystem acts as a brake on the SNS, managing the "feed and breed" system and helping the body gently return from arousal to relaxation. It's also the most ancient threat-response system in our bodies and one we share with reptiles and other mammals. Anatomically, the dorsal vagal consists of a nerve pathway that connects the brain stem to the organs situated below the diaphragm, especially those associated with digestion and reproduction and the muscles that anchor these organs in place.

Figure 6: Vagus Nerve

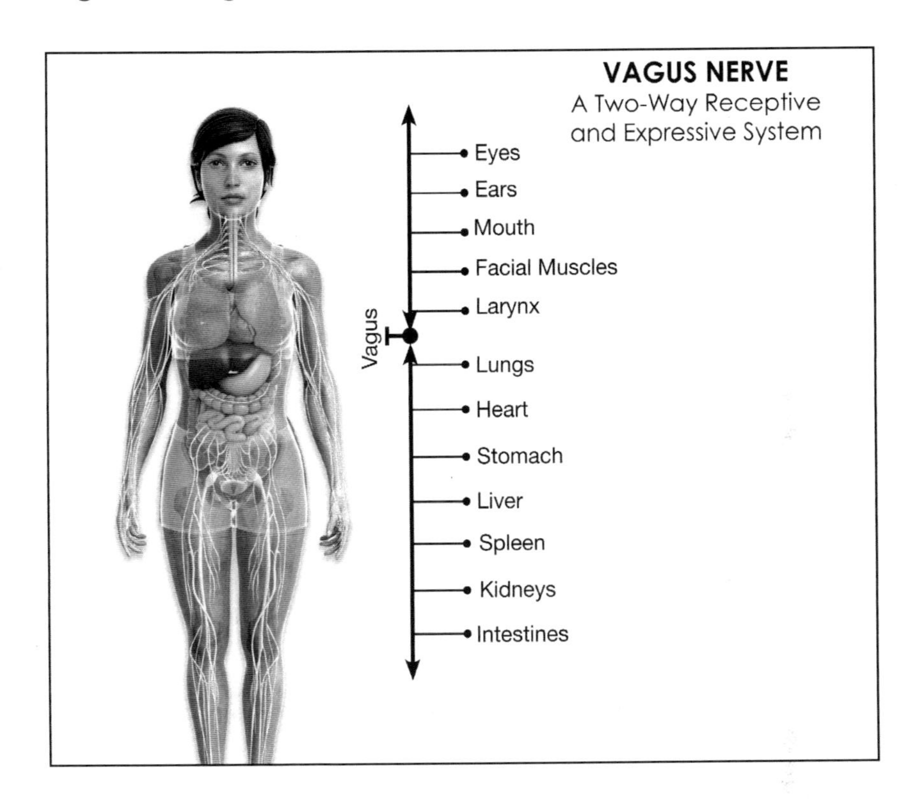

The dorsal vagal system first evolved in simple organisms that passively absorbed nutrients from the rich broth of dissolved organic compounds and gases found in the prehistoric ocean. Lacking organs and muscles for locomotion, these simple creatures never developed a sympathetic nervous system or the option to fight or flee. Instead, their defensive systems were focused entirely on preserving their energy reserves so they could recover as quickly as possible when the threat had ceased. For this reasons, the DV is sometimes referred to as the "passive defense system."

The DV system is now understood to control the third possible response to a perceived threat: freezing. We can see this survival strategy at work when we observe animals responding to danger by becoming immobilized. This is often described as the "deer in the headlights" phenomenon.

Consider the case of a driver trapped in his vehicle and unable to move after a car accident. His dorsal vagal system immediately springs into action, slowing his heart rate, reducing his blood pressure, and preserving his energy resources for the key organ systems necessary for survival. If this inhibitory response is severe enough, however, the suppression of his heart and circulatory system may cause him to go into shock and lose consciousness; potentially with fatal consequences.

Our driver's amygdala may also respond by creating a powerful emotional memory of the accident and its aftermath. This memory—stored below conscious awareness—might include all of the sensory impressions surrounding the accident along with the signals of biological shutdown induced by DV activation. Consequently, whenever the memory is triggered in the future, he may re-experience some of the classic physiological and psychological manifestations of the freeze response, including such symptoms as:

- Dissociation
- Paralysis of thought or action
- Emotional numbing and psychological disengagement

If the stress evoking the freeze response is chronic, our driver may attempt to manage these symptoms by self-medicating (e.g., drugs and alcohol), escapism (e.g., web surfing and video games), self-soothing (e.g., cutting), or by distancing himself from others and avoiding activities he may have previously enjoyed.

Figure 7: The "Triune" Threat-Response System

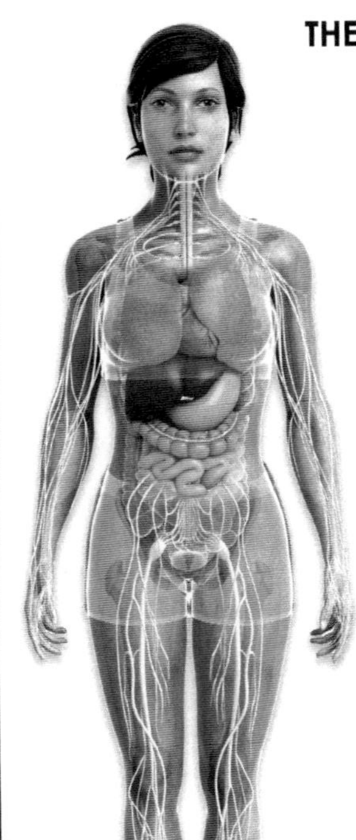

Our Social Engagement System

The third component of our threat-response system evolved most recently and is found only in humans. The ventral vagal (VV) subsystem is the second branch of the parasympathetic nervous system and the one that most directly reflects our status as social beings with biological imperatives to form mutually beneficial relationships. Anatomically, the ventral vagal system connects the brain stem to the organs above the diaphragm, (e.g., the heart, lungs, etc.) and to the muscles of the face and head. As part of the parasympathetic nervous system, the ventral vagal system furnishes similar capabilities for relaxing our bodies and suppressing the fight-or-flight response generated by the sympathetic nervous system and the freeze response generated by the dorsal vagal system. However, unlike either of these systems, it operates through the medium of face-to-face communications. For this reason, the VV is sometimes referred to as the "social engagement system."

If the eyes are the portal to the soul, then the face is the window to the threat-response system and our voices are the music of engagement. When the ventral vagal system is dominant, we feel safe, centered, and secure. We convey this through our facial muscles by smiling and maintaining appropriate eye contact. We do the same with our tone of voice, speaking in a relaxed and rhythmic way that eschews choppy or staccato phrases. Think of a mother singing a lullaby to her baby or the sound of two lovers cooing their endearments. We hear differently too, focusing our attention on the person speaking to us and losing awareness of background noise.

Today, we know that the profound sense of well-being we experience when we establish a secure connection with another human being is caused by the release of oxytocin, a powerful neurotransmitter secreted by our pituitary gland. Recent research has also shown that oxytocin can be effective in preventing survivors of recent trauma from developing PTSD symptoms. All of these stress reduction responses are mediated by the ventral vagal system.

When we encounter stress, humans naturally turn to each other for comfort and support. If we see a friendly face, the ventral vagal system activates to calm us. If we encounter someone whose face and voice communicate anxiety or distress, we may become aroused and infected by their stress. This is the

Figure 8: Polyvagal Theory

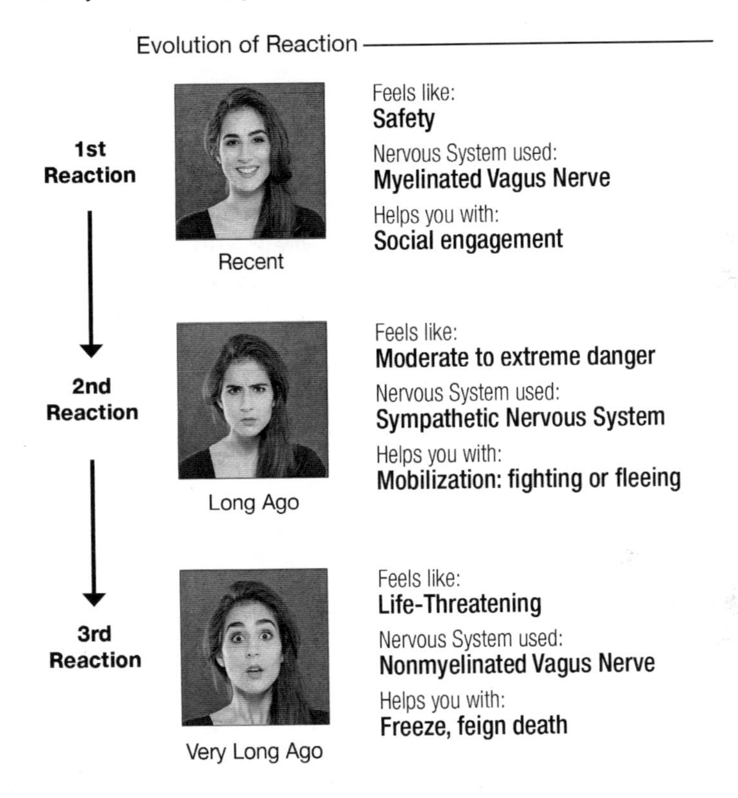

biological basis for the kind of environmentally caused stress my patient Joshua experienced through repeated exposure to his father's traumatic memories.

As shown in Figure 8, our passive defense, fight-or-flight, and social engagement systems come online in a consistent, evolutionarily defined sequence. If we perceive danger, we look first to our fellow humans for support. If we find it, we relax. If not, our SNS takes over and we attempt to fight or flee. If we're prevented from fighting or fleeing, then our earliest evolved system takes control. The entire process is entirely outside of our conscious awareness and occurs almost instantaneously within a scant 10–15 milliseconds.

The Biological Effects of Chronic Stress

Our threat-response systems can become dangerously over-extended when we encounter stress on an ongoing basis. When this occurs, the SNS can get stuck in the "on" position, plunging us into a near-constant state of agitation and overarousal. Our bodies become like cars driven with both the accelerator and brake pedals mashed to the floorboards. We spend our days "red-lined," going fast but getting nowhere as we burn out our engines. There is considerable research pointing to chronic stress as the root cause of many diseases, psychological problems, and immune system dysfunctions.

Dysregulation like this can become a vicious cycle. Any stressful situation we encounter may provoke a full-scale fight, flight, or freeze response. Driving to work, we fly into a rage when someone cuts us off. When presented with a challenge, we find ourselves unable to act. Failing to deal effectively with minor setbacks, we become even more stressed. Our innate capabilities for intelligence, creativity, emotional connection, and considered judgment are sharply degraded. Our health and well-being are endangered. We live our lives on a hair trigger, ready to explode or implode at the slightest provocation.

These physiological responses have very real consequences for millions of individuals, including my patients Mark, Jill, and Joshua. All three were contending to varying degrees with dysregulation of their threat-response system. Jill became dysregulated by the chronic stress she experienced growing up in a dysfunctional home. Mark became dysregulated in his medical practice by observing the pain and suffering his patients experienced as a result of illness and death. Joshua became dysregulated by chronic exposure to his father's chronic SNS activation. Gradually and insidiously, the effects of this dysregulation worsened until it poisoned their lives.

Fortunately, no one has to be victimized by their physiological responses or live a diminished life due to chronic stress. We can overcome the reflexive activation of our threat-response systems and learn to bring them under conscious control. When we encounter challenging situations, we can learn to see them in perspective and react with intelligence, judgment, and creativity. We can feel comfort in our bodies as we think and act with maximum efficiency. In biological terms, we can learn to overcome dysregulation and restore ventral vagal system dominance. Once we do this, we can eliminate the negative effects of stress, optimize our health and well-being, and live productive, satisfying lives infused with intentionality, inspiration, and meaning. In every moment of our lives, we can evolve and grow.

CHAPTER 3

Beginning the Journey from Trauma to Transformation

> *"Make the most of yourself...*
> *for that is all there is of you."*
>
> — RALPH WALDO EMERSON —

As we've seen, stress is not a ubiquitous feature of our environment. It is not a heavy yoke imposed on us by the outside world or a disease we contract through exposure to a pathogen. Stress is simply our own biological response to a perceived threat, a response we can learn to moderate and control with practice.

We've traced the neural and hormonal pathways that collectively comprise our primitive threat detection and response systems and shown how they operate largely outside of our conscious awareness. We've demonstrated how chronic stress—in the form of primary, secondary, and environmental trauma—can push these systems into dysregulation. We've also explained why the near-constant overactivation of our fight, flight, and freeze responses can be so destructive to our health, our relationships, our performance, and our satisfaction with our lives.

If this were the end of the story, our prospects for a stress-free life would seem very bleak indeed. Fortunately, biology is not destiny. We can learn to overcome dysregulation and restore a healthy balance to our threat detection systems, eliminating our vulnerability to stress in the process. As we emerge from our entrenched patterns of reflexive reactivity, we can become free to behave in ways that are consistent with our ethics, values, and aspirations. We can learn to control our reactions and choose our responses. As Viktor Frankl has said, *"In our response lies our growth and our freedom."* Increasingly, we can bring the full weight of our skills, intelligence, and creativity to bear in every sphere of our lives. We can face challenges with new energy and confidence. In short, we can become our best selves.

What would it take to bring about such a fundamental transformation? What strategies and methods would we employ? How would we put them into practice?

Any meaningful approach to eliminating the scourge of chronic stress must satisfy a number of critical requirements. First and foremost, it should employ methods that anyone can learn to apply with a little practice and dedication. Buddhist monks spend decades mastering advanced meditation techniques that enable them to control their heart rate, suppress their involuntary startle responses, and "light up" different parts of their brains at will. However, few of us possess the time or discipline to devote ourselves in this way. Our approach should empower us to reduce the impact of stress on our lives as quickly and efficiently as possible.

We know that the stress response operates along a continuum. Some of us are contending with the relatively mild levels of arousal associated with daily stressors such as getting stuck in traffic when we're late for work. At the other end of the spectrum, some of us are struggling with the panic attacks and intrusive thoughts evoked by full-blown PTSD. Therefore, the stress reduction strategy we choose should work effectively for everyone, regardless of where we find ourselves on the stress continuum. And we should be able to apply it in every stage and aspect of our lives.

Of course, we cannot and should not ignore the painful learning that caused us to become dysregulated in the first place. However, we shouldn't have to excavate and wallow in every trauma we've ever experienced in order to heal. Instead, our stress elimination regimen should gently empower us to make choices today—in the present moment—that reflect our most cherished goals and aspirations for the future. The techniques we use should help us move beyond dependency and victimhood to a sense of pride and self-reliance. In short, we should be inspired to look forward with hope, not backwards with anger and sorrow.

Introducing Forward-Facing Trauma Therapy

Forward-Facing Trauma Therapy (FFTT) represents a new approach to managing and eliminating stress that is explicitly designed to address all of these requirements and more.

- Restoring homeostasis. We can't just flip a switch and reboot our brains into a state of harmony and homeostasis. However, we can learn to consciously activate our parasympathetic nervous system whenever we sense the sympathetic nervous system roaring into action. We won't be able to entirely prevent SNS activation (nor would we want to when confronted with a real threat to our safety). But we will be able to rein it in rapidly and effectively by sensing when it begins to run amok. In Chapter 4, we'll begin developing the foundational skills of self-regulation that make this possible.

- Aligning our behavior with our values. In the throes of SNS dominance, we're much more likely to lose control and behave in ways that are, at best, ineffective, and, at worst, destructive to ourselves and others. Reducing the frequency and intensity of these episodes is certainly a worthwhile goal in itself. However, an equally important goal is learning to act in accordance with our ideals, values, and principles. The first step in achieving that goal is deciding who we are and who we want to be. In Chapter 5, we'll begin a process of self-exploration that culminates in the development of a written covenant and code of honor that will help us navigate the vicissitudes of life with intentionality and purpose.
- Identifying and managing our triggers. When we experience chronic stress, we can enter a state of hypervigilance in which our threat detection systems are always running on overdrive. In this state, anything we unconsciously associate with painful past experiences—a sound, a smell, a physical sensation—can plunge us into a full-scale fight, flight, or freeze response. As a result, we may be triggered dozens or even hundreds of times each day. In Chapter 6, we'll learn how to identify and negate the power of our triggers by applying our newly honed skills of self-regulation and intentionality.

We can see this process at work in Figure 9.

Figure 9: FFTT and the Virtuous Circle

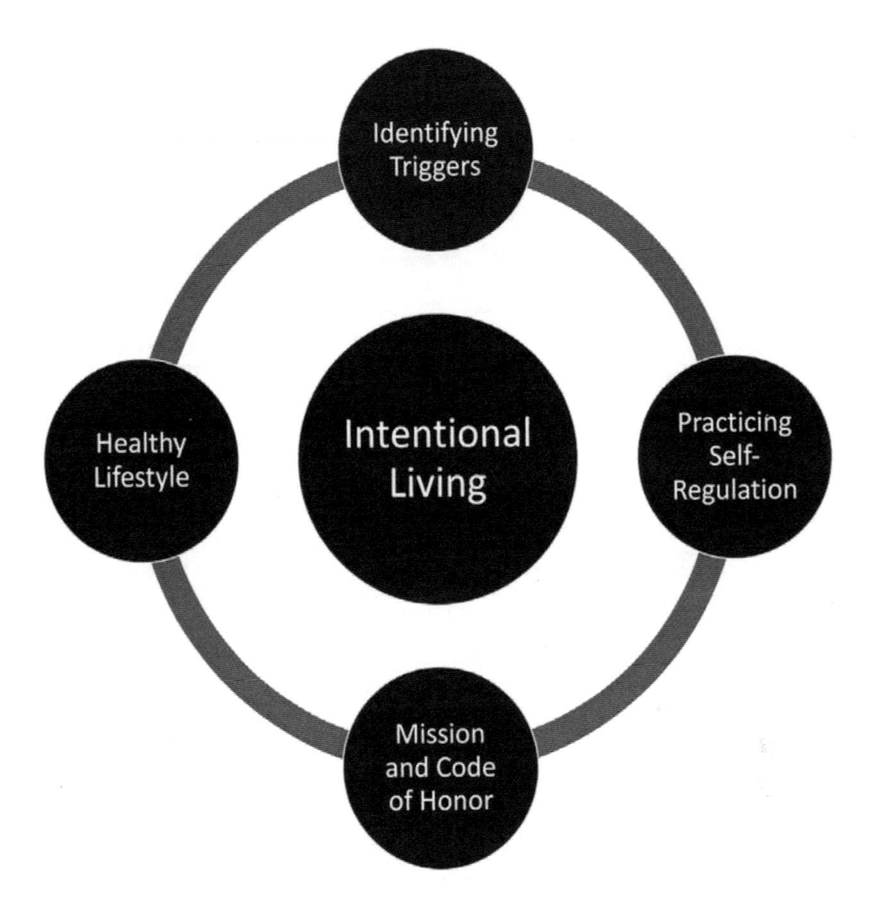

FFTT vs. Traditional Psychotherapy

The primary goal of traditional trauma-oriented psychotherapy is to reduce and eliminate symptoms, not to provide an ethical or moral framework for living with intentionality. In contrast, the primary goal of FFTT is to develop resilience and the capacity to live meaningful, principle-based lives. As it happens, the techniques we employ in FFTT help us accomplish both goals at the same time.

Like other forms of psychotherapy, FFTT provides a structured approach to treatment that can be practiced effectively by trained therapists in the clinical setting. However, there are some essential differences.

In many forms of psychotherapy—especially those based on cognitive-behavioral techniques—there is an implicit assumption that psychological problems are caused or exacerbated by the client's faulty perceptions and skewed thought processes. Thus, the therapist's job is conceived, in part, as helping clients develop the insight needed to deconstruct these patterned responses so they can more effectively navigate their lives. When practiced by a warm and empathetic therapist, this process can produce a raft of meaningful cognitions and an array of new skills that the client is excited to put into practice in their day-to-day lives. All too often, however, these apparent gains evaporate instantly as soon as the client leaves the therapist's office.

When confronted by stress, the client immediately loses access to the high-level brain structures where their insights reside, reverting instantly to the primitive thinking patterns and behaviors associated with their outmatched threat-response systems. This ultimately becomes a double whammy to their confidence and hopes for change. Filled with shame and doubt, they may ask themselves, "What's wrong with me that I can't apply what I've tried so hard to learn when it really matters?" This destructive self-perception is further compounded when they return to therapy to report their "failure," only to be told they must simply "work harder." When this pattern inevitably repeats, many clients lose hope and exit therapy prematurely. In truth, however, it's not the client who has failed. The failure lies with a therapeutic approach that requires clients to utilize logic and abstract reasoning when the high-level brain structures that make this possible have been switched off by their threat detection system.

In FFTT, the therapist doesn't function as a doctor whose job is to "heal" the client, but rather as a coach who assists the client in removing impediments to their maturational trajectory. FFTT practitioners recognize that it is the underlying threat-response system that is causing our primitive thoughts and reactions and that these will naturally wither away in the course of restoring homeostasis.

Depending on your level of dysregulation, you may find that certain triggers are so powerful and primal that you're plunged into reactivity despite your best efforts to self-regulate. This is most often the result of traumatic learning that causes the SNS to spike so quickly and intensely that the space between stimulus and response collapses. In these cases, treatment methods such as Eye Movement Reprocessing and Desensitization (EMDR) can be utilized by a skilled therapist to reduce the intensity of your triggers until they are no longer so overwhelming. Once this occurs, FFTT and self-regulation can resume productively. However, many of us will be able to employ FFTT successfully without ever visiting a therapist's office. Thus, FFTT can accurately be described both as a clinical treatment methodology and as a self-help model for achieving lasting personal transformation.

The beneficial effects of Forward-Facing Trauma Therapy will accrue more quickly as you are able to adopt healthier strategies than the maladaptive behaviors you may have previously employed to manage your stress and soothe your anxiety.

In FFTT, we emphasize the importance of a healthy lifestyle in promoting growth and healing. That means getting plenty of sleep, eating a healthy diet, exercising regularly, and participating in a spiritual tradition that gives meaning to your life and connects you to your community. All of these are essential to promoting growth and becoming your best self.

Since opening my practice in 1990, I've helped thousands of patients experience the benefits of FFTT. Many report dramatic reductions in their stress levels within a matter of weeks. I've also conducted workshops across the U.S., training hundreds of thousands of therapists in the techniques described in this book. We still have much to learn about the biology of stress and why FFTT is so effective. But, simply put, FFTT works.

Forward-Facing Trauma Therapy: Is It Right for You?

The self-regulation techniques you'll be applying in FFTT are easy to learn, but they must be practiced diligently every day for the rest of your life. This may seem a daunting prospect to those of us seeking a "magic bullet" solution to our problems. However, FFTT should be viewed as a process, not an endpoint. Its benefits are incalculable, but they require effort and dedication. If you're not ready to commit to change, then FFTT is not for you.

You should not try practicing FFTT on your own if you're contending with severe depression, PTSD, an anxiety disorder, or a substance use disorder, or if you're taking medications to treat these and other mental health conditions. Instead, you should work with a trained professional who can coordinate your care and utilize appropriate evidence-based interventions to reduce the severity of your symptoms and help you stabilize. You can't practice FFTT productively when you're in crisis.

We should also never overlook the possibility that your stress and its symptoms may have an organic cause. Consult your physician to make sure you have a clean bill of health before starting FFTT. Keep in mind that while FFTT cannot cure disease, it can play a major role in healing by enhancing your resilience and dissipating some of the stress you may be experiencing due to poor health.

As always, the first step in solving a problem is to admit you have one. Take a moment now to fill out this brief questionnaire.

FFTT Self-Evaluation Worksheet

	Yes	No
1. My life is so stressful that I often feel overwhelmed.		
2. I often behave in ways that I regret later.		
3. I frequently say and do things that hurt people I care about.		
4. There are situations and people that push my buttons and make me crazy, so I avoid them and keep to myself as much as possible.		
5. I feel empty and unsatisfied with my life.		
6. I've tried to change but found it impossible on my own.		
7. I feel controlled by other people.		
8. I would like to have more meaning in my life.		
9. I want to do a better job of being true to my principles and living with integrity.		
10. I think I may be suffering from primary, secondary, or environmental trauma.		

If you scored four or more "Yes" answers, then you should seriously consider FFTT.

Are you ready to escape the vicious, self-defeating cycle of stress, reactivity, and acting out that only leads to more stress, more reactivity, and more acting out? Are you ready to find new meaning in your life? If so, you're ready to embark on your journey from trauma to transformation. You're ready to begin practicing Forward-Facing Trauma Therapy.

CHAPTER 4

Interoception and Self-Regulation

"(W)e all begin life in a state of relaxed and joyful bliss."

— HARVILLE HENDRIX—

It's the spring of 1995 and I'm lying on the floor next to my then wife Janet and 50 other couples. We're taking part in a guided meditation led by Dr. Harville Hendrix, co-founder of Imago Therapy and author of the best-selling book *Getting the Love You Want: A Guide for Couples.* I'm starting to feel a bit sleepy as he gently urges us in a sonorous voice to "...picture yourself moving with relaxed joyfulness."

I'm not exactly sure what he means, but I'm doing my best to cooperate until his next words send me bolt upright, confused and agitated to the point of near panic. "Relaxed joyfulness is our natural state," he has just told us. Looking around the room, I notice that everyone else is smiling in agreement. Why am I the only one who finds his words so disturbing?

For those of us whose lives have been powerfully shaped by severe stress and childhood trauma, the claim that our natural state is relaxed joyfulness sounds like a cruel joke. We often distrust and dislike our bodies, feeling that they have somehow betrayed us. *Our* natural state is one of tension and hypervigilance, the very antithesis of relaxed joyfulness. Our past painful learning is evident in our chronically clenched muscles and rigid, inflexible joints. In biological terms, we live in a near-constant state of sympathetic nervous system (SNS) dominance.

Some 20 years later, I have come to understand that a state of relaxed joyfulness is not only possible; it's inevitable when we perfect the skills of self-regulation. In this chapter, you'll learn to pay attention to your body on a moment-to-moment basis so that you can instantly recognize and respond to the muscular constriction that signals SNS activation. You'll start to notice how relaxing these muscles can quickly return your body—and your mind—to the restful and healing state of parasympathetic nervous system (PNS) dominance.

In subsequent chapters, you'll learn to apply your newly honed self-regulation skills to your activities of daily living (ADL). This will be particularly important when you're triggered into re-experiencing your past painful learning. Finally, as stress loses its grip on your body and mind, you'll start developing a new capacity to choose how you want to live your life. You'll be empowered to act in accordance with your core values and beliefs. You'll discover that relaxed joyfulness truly is your natural state and the foundation for a rich and meaningful life.

Interoception + Relaxation Response = Self-Regulation

Self-regulation is easy to learn but difficult to master. You can see this for yourself by trying out this simple exercise. Sit down in a comfortable chair, close your eyes, and begin focusing on the sensations within your body. Scan up and down from head to toe, searching for tense muscles. Pay close attention to tension hot spots, such as your neck, shoulders, jaw, and stomach.

This process of consciously shifting your attention away from the outside world to the inner world of your body is what we mean when we use the medical term "interoception," which is sometimes referred to more colloquially as "bodifulness." Interoception is quite different from mindfulness, in which we simply observe our thoughts without judging or engaging them. With interoception, our goal is to become fluent in the silent but equally eloquent language of our bodies—to begin to know ourselves from the inside out. Interoception is the process of making a comfortable place to live within our bodies.

Let's return now to our exercise. Resume scanning your body from head to toe. Whenever you find a tense muscle, consciously relax it until your whole body is as floppy and droopy as a wet noodle. Notice how calm, relaxed, and centered you feel. Congratulations! You've just performed your first official act of self-regulation. Biologically speaking, you've restored yourself to the healing state of PNS dominance.

Self-regulation works because it makes use of a biological reflex first identified in the late 1940s by Joseph Wolpe, a South African psychiatrist. At the time, Wolpe was serving as a medical officer and treating World War II combat veterans for what was then referred to as "war neurosis" but is today recognized as PTSD. Wolpe quickly became disillusioned with the treatment methods in vogue at the time, which combined the use of the drug sodium pentathol ("truth serum") and Freudian psychodynamics. Not only did this approach fail to help most of his patients, he later reported, it actually seemed to exacerbate the symptoms of many others.

Instead, Wolpe began to draw on the results of his own animal studies with cats as well as experiments by Pavlov and other learning theorists who were exploring the physiological basis of the fear response. This research showed that the intensity of the physiological arousal caused by fear and anxiety could be systematically controlled using a variety of classical conditioning techniques. For example, Wolpe found that he could inhibit a cat's conditioned fear response to a stimulus by offering it food. In effect, the pleasurable feeling was interfering with the fearful response. When Wolpe applied this method of "reciprocal inhibition" to his clinical practice, the results were extraordinary. Reciprocal inhibition—more broadly defined as confronting fear-inducing situations with a relaxed body—is the core methodology for virtually all effective trauma treatments, including FFTT.

Over the ensuing decades, Wolpe continued his clinical work and research into the treatment of anxiety and phobias, publishing numerous books and scientific articles and becoming closely identified with the technique of "systematic desensitization," which to this day remains the most widespread and effective method for treating patients with phobias.

Herbert Benson, MD, a cardiologist and researcher at Harvard Medical School, drew on Wolpe's work in an effort to ameliorate the physical symptoms of extreme stress that his patients typically experienced during the painful and often protracted process of diagnosis and treatment. In 1975, he published his seminal work, the best-selling book *The Relaxation Response*. There, Dr. Benson shared the results of his research showing how relaxation counteracts the fight-or-fight response while helping the body to heal.

"The relaxation response is a physical state of deep rest that changes the physical and emotional responses to stress... and is the opposite of the fight-or-flight response."[11]

— HERBERT BENSON —

Since publishing his groundbreaking book, Dr. Benson has won widespread acclaim for his pioneering work in the field of mind/body medicine, bringing scientific rigor to the study of the intimate connection between our mental states and our physical health. Today, he serves as mind body medicine professor of medicine at Harvard Medical School and director emeritus of the Benson-Henry Institute for Mind Body Medicine at Massachusetts General Hospital.

Dr. Benson's core insight—that our bodies cannot simultaneously be relaxed and SNS activated—explains why reciprocal inhibition has become a mainstay of almost every form of trauma therapy. In the Trauma Resiliency Model (TRM), for example, patients learn to identify two sets of bodily sensations: one associated with stressful or traumatic memories and another associated with memories that are pleasurable and uplifting. Then, whenever they feel distress associated with painful learning, patients invoke the positive memories, along with various relaxation techniques to oppose and overcome the stress response. Gradually, over time, the balance between the stress and relaxation response changes until patients finally succeed in returning their bodies to homeostasis.

Like TRM and other state-of-the-art trauma treatments, Forward-Facing Trauma Therapy utilizes interoception and the relaxation response to overcome the dysregulation caused by chronic stress and trauma. However, FFTT does much more than this.

- TRM and other trauma therapies are primarily practiced in the clinical setting. In contrast, most people find that they can utilize FFTT techniques without ever seeing a therapist.
- FFTT utilizes relaxation methods that can be applied without anyone noticing. This is essential in meeting our goal to eliminate stress while interacting with the people, places, and situations we encounter every day. In contrast, approaches like TRM often utilize the meditation-oriented relaxation techniques Dr. Benson first described in *The Relaxation Response*. Typically, you must find a secluded space where you can sit quietly and practice mindfulness for 10–20 minutes while using a "mental device" such as a repeated sound or mantra. You would hardly expect to apply such methods while arguing with your spouse or participating in a business meeting!
- Chronic dysregulation causes us to feel and act as if we're frozen in time, locked in an endless cycle of self-defeating behaviors that undermine us and distress those around us. Approaches like TRM can be extremely helpful in reducing the speed and severity of our reflexive transition from relaxation to fight-or-flight mode. This is what Viktor Frankl was referring to when he wrote, "Between stimulus and response there is a space."

Like TRM, Forward-Facing Trauma Therapy is very effective in creating this space. But what then? No other stress model or treatment methodology I've come across addresses the moral and ethical dimensions of our newfound ability to choose how to behave during these moments of clarity. Only FFTT provides us with the forward-looking ethical framework needed to help us navigate our lives with purpose and meaning. As Frankl so eloquently stated, "In that space is our power to choose our response. In our response lies our growth and our freedom."

Internal vs. External Locus of Control

In my workshops, I'll often follow up my demonstration of self-regulation by asking attendees to try the opposite experiment. "Close your eyes and think about the last time you felt really stressed," I'll say. "Now, tell me how your bodies are reacting." Invariably, almost everyone responds that they're feeling their jaws clench and their muscles contract. Next, I'll ask, "Who do you think is doing all of that squeezing? Are you enjoying it?"

The questions seem so absurd that most attendees start laughing. However, the point I'm making, albeit humorously, is a serious one. When we attribute stress to our environment—to people and situations outside ourselves—we're making a grave error. We're relinquishing our freedom to chart our own destinies. After all, it's not the outside world that's squeezing our muscles and making us miserable. *We're doing it to ourselves.* FFTT is unique in helping us regain control of the one thing we truly own; our power to choose how we react to the people and situations around us. In technical terms, FFTT enables us to shift from an *external* locus of control—one of powerlessness and victimhood—to an *internal* locus of control in which we are empowered and free.

Learning to Trigger the Relaxation Response

Earlier, I used the wet noodle exercise to illustrate how easy it is to learn self-regulation and how the process occurs in two stages:

1. Scanning your body to identify stress points (interoception).
2. Purposefully relaxing your muscles (to evoke the relaxation response).

In practice, however, the wet noodle method leaves much to be desired. The true power of self-regulation lies in our ability to apply it while remaining fully engaged in our daily lives. This is why I always emphasize that self-regulation is easy to learn but difficult to master. It will never become an automatic, unconscious process like driving. If you want to live stress-free, you'll have to perform it consciously and consistently for the rest of your life. However, you do have a good deal of flexibility when it comes to choosing a relaxation method that works best for you. Let's explore what I believe to be the most efficient method first.

As I described in Chapter 3, the dorsal branch of the vagus nerve connects the brain stem to the organs situated below the diaphragm. When we encounter stress, the nearby muscles reflexively contract, squeezing the vagus nerve and causing it to emit a chaotic series of "Help! I'm in danger!" signals to our sympathetic nervous system. In turn, the SNS responds by causing our muscles to contract in preparation for fighting or fleeing. This creates a destructive feedback loop between the vagus and the SNS that causes our stress response to continue escalating long after the perceived danger has passed.

Eventually, our threat detection systems become set at the redline level of hypervigilance, leaving us in a chronic state of dysregulation.

Therefore, one of the quickest and most efficient ways to overcome SNS activation is to relax the core muscles pressing against the dorsal vagus. When we do so, reciprocal inhibition forces the SNS to disengage, allowing the feed and breed system to rapidly restore us to PNS dominance. However, this method of stimulating the relaxation response doesn't work for everyone. Children who grow up in a culture of fear, shame, and violence often respond by learning to tune out the unpleasant sensations of stress they carry in their chronically constricted muscles. As adults, they understand intellectually that they possess the same core muscles as everyone else, but they may be unable to readily feel or locate them easily.

Consider the case of "Callie," a 29-year-old systems engineer for a large multinational corporation. Thanks to her extraordinary talent and work ethic, Callie completed a meteoric rise to become head of her department in only three years. However, her new role in management was proving to be more stressful and debilitating than she had anticipated. When I first met her, Callie was getting by on only two to three hours of sleep and consuming less than 800 calories a day, usually in the form of sugar and caffeine. She was tense, miserable, and pessimistic about the future.

During our first session, I introduced Callie to the core tenets of Forward-Facing Trauma Therapy and explained the connection between the distressing symptoms she was experiencing and the dysregulation that was being created by her amped-up stress response. At the end of the session, she agreed to try relaxing her body whenever she encountered a perceived threat at work. Callie left the session bright with hope that her life was about to change for the better.

However, when Callie arrived for our next session, I could see that she was depressed and irritable. Despite her best intentions, she had been so distracted by the moment-to-moment pressures of her job that she had gone almost the entire week without checking in with her body. As a result, she spent the week "stressed out," indulging her tendency to treat colleagues in an aggressive and condescending manner. They retaliated in kind, ratcheting up her stress levels even higher as the vicious cycle repeated over and over again.

To solve this conundrum, I instructed Callie to close her eyes and visualize several of the most stressful situations she had encountered during the previous week. I then asked her, "What do you notice happening in your body RIGHT NOW?" Callie reported that she felt tightness in her abdominal and gluteus muscles. I asked her to clench these muscles as hard as she could for five seconds and then release the tension to stimulate the relaxation response. I encouraged her to repeat this exercise five more times until she was able to consistently "find" these muscles and relax them while visualizing stressful situations. By the end of the session, she had completely regained her equanimity. As homework, I asked her to continue practicing this interoception exercise while noting down the work situations she found most stressful and considering what each of these "triggers" might have in common.

A week later, a very different Callie entered my office. She proudly reported that she had been able to keep her muscles relaxed in more than half of the stressful situations she had encountered the prior week. As a result, her interactions with colleagues had gone more smoothly and her stress level at work had plummeted. Callie now regarded her abdominal and gluteus muscles as a kind of friendly "early warning" system that allowed her to control her stress before it overwhelmed her. She expressed amazement that something as simple as purposefully relaxing her muscles could have such a rapid and decisive impact on her quality of life. She also felt far more hopeful about her prospects for continued improvement in the months to come.

Some clients need to employ multiple methods to achieve self-regulation. This was the case with "James," a 42-year-old physician who practices emergency medicine at a large suburban hospital. I first encountered James during the course of my work helping physicians develop professional resilience. Over the past year, James' behavior had become increasingly erratic. He was referred to me for therapeutic intervention after an incident in which he threw a surgical instrument at a nurse during an emergency procedure. James' home life was also suffering due to his frequent angry outbursts, which provoked fearful reactions from his wife and children that left him feeling alienated and confused. As a result, he avoided family activities and kept to himself as much as possible.

My first session with James began the usual way. I outlined the role of the sympathetic and parasympathetic nervous systems in regulating our responses to stress and explained how this process can go awry, especially for physicians and other medical professionals who are charged with making life-and-death decisions every day. James listened with a palpable and barely concealed impatience. Like many of the physicians I've worked with, he was undoubtedly thinking, "What can a mental health professional teach me about the autonomic nervous system? NOTHING!"

However, James soon had his own "light bulb" moment in which he was able to connect his abstract understanding of human physiology to his personal experience of stress-induced dysregulation. At this point, I walked him through the same process I had used with Callie. In short order, James was able to locate and then relax the muscles below his diaphragm while visualizing some of the stressful events that had provoked his meltdowns. By the end of the session, he felt ready to apply self-regulation at work.

I met James again about a month later during a follow-up visit to California. Overall, he said, things were getting better. His relationship with his wife and children had improved considerably and he was now taking greater pleasure in family activities. He seemed calmer and more centered, thanks to his practice of self-regulation at home. However, he was still struggling through his shifts in the ER.

Much like Callie, James was continually overwhelmed by the demands of his job. He was so busy, he often forgot to eat lunch or go to the bathroom, much less take time to monitor and relax his muscles. He expressed disappointment and confusion that no matter how hard he tried, he was unable to apply the self-regulation he was using so successfully at home in his work environment.

Recognizing that James needed another "tool in his self-regulation toolbox," I taught him another relaxation technique to supplement the core relaxation method he had already mastered. The peripheral vision technique was first developed by the U.S. military to help snipers improve their shooting accuracy. Trainees would be instructed to attend to their peripheral vision for ten seconds before peering through the rifle scope at their target. This enabled them to relax their muscles, allowing for greater stability while inhibiting the micro-movements of arms and hands that can sharply degrade shooting accuracy. James mastered the technique on his first try and resolved to put it into practice shortly thereafter.

I didn't see James again until I returned to California several months later to attend an emergency medicine convention. When he first came over to say hello, I barely recognized the robust man who stood before me. The pale, nervous, underweight patient I had worked with months before had been transformed. He was now working out, eating healthily, sleeping well, and enjoying his life. He looked and sounded like a new man.

James attributed his success to the peripheral vision relaxation method, which had enabled him to "get a lever into the space between stimulus and response." (James had become as big a fan of Viktor Frankl and his work as I am.) After diligently practicing the peripheral vision method for several weeks, he became increasingly attuned to his body while at work. Eventually, he was able to discard the peripheral vision method entirely and respond to stress by simply releasing the muscles in his core. As a result, his stress level dropped precipitously and he was able to derive a newfound sense of fulfillment and enjoyment from his career as a healer and helper. Within three years, James was promoted to medical director of the emergency department from which he had nearly been fired. Self-regulation had saved both his career and his marriage.

Many Roads to the Summit

When I first began studying and later teaching self-regulation in the mid 1990s, I focused exclusively on the relaxation methods I had taught to Callie and James. I told my clients and workshop participants that these were the only viable ways to eliminate stress and dysregulation. However, I now recognize that self-regulation can be achieved using a variety of techniques and work closely with each patient to find the method or methods that will be most effective for them.

Despite their apparent differences, all of these techniques share a common feature: they harness interoception and the conscious release of muscle tension to stimulate the relaxation response. Here are two more methods for you to consider.

- Diaphragmatic or "belly" breathing. One of the effects of SNS activation is a dramatic change in our breathing patterns. As we prepare to fight or flee, we fuel our muscles with oxygen by breathing rapidly and shallowly, using our chest muscles rather than our diaphragms to draw air in and out. The reverse is also true. When we engage in rapid chest breathing, our threat detection systems may interpret this as a danger signal and react by invoking a full-fledged fight-or-flight response. Diaphragmatic breathing acts as a counterweight to this SNS activation, utilizing reciprocal inhibition to trigger the relaxation response and return us to PNS dominance.
- Soft palate relaxation. Like the core relaxation method, this technique directly counteracts vagus nerve stimulation to restore parasympathetic dominance. However, it acts upon the branch of the vagal system that originates

at the soft palate near the roof of the mouth rather than the branch that terminates in the muscles of the core.

In Worksheet 1, you'll find detailed "step-by-step" instructions for performing the self-regulation techniques I've described in this chapter. I encourage you to experiment with all of them until you find the ones that work best for you.

Next Steps

You may find it hard to believe that something as simple as self-regulation has the power to transform your life in ways that are profoundly positive and far-reaching. However, after teaching this essential skill to thousands of clients and tens of thousands of therapists, I can assure you that this is true. The more you practice these simple skills, the more attuned you'll become to your body and its powerful distress signals. Increasingly, you'll be able to make fine, moment-to-moment adjustments to the level of energy you bring to each challenge in your life until you are consistently operating within the optimal energy zone described by the Yerkes-Dodson Law.

Self-regulation will allow you to create the precious space Frankl wrote about between stimulus (perceived danger) and response (SNS activation) in which you're free to make rational, principled choices about how you want to respond to the world around you. Of course, freedom comes at a cost. You must commit yourself to attaining mastery, performing self-regulation assiduously every 2–3 minutes for the rest of your life. It truly is simple, but not easy.

In Chapter 5, I'll show you how to develop the moral and ethical framework you'll need to live a principled, intentional life by creating your personal covenant and code of honor. Then, in Chapter 6, we'll start putting it all together by identifying the people and situations that trigger you into dysregulation and applying self-regulation every time this occurs.

The thousands of patients I've treated and hundreds of therapists I've trained in Forward-Facing Trauma Therapy can testify to the power of self-regulation in transforming lives and eliminating stress. But don't take my word for it—try it out for yourself and see what happens. Start by experimenting with all of the relaxation methods described in Worksheet 1. Next, choose the ones that work best for you and practice them as directed in Worksheet 2. You'll be amazed to discover that a state of relaxed and joyful bliss can truly be yours with a little practice and persistence. After all, you have nothing to lose and everything to gain.

WORKSHEET 1:

How to Invoke the Relaxation Response

Method 1: Relaxation of the Core Muscles

In this exercise, your goal is to locate and then relax constricted muscles in your core.

1. Sit down comfortably and place a hand under each side of your bottom.
2. Now feel for the pointed bones that you're sitting upon. These mark the lower boundary of your core.
3. Next, find and touch the two bony points just above your waist on the right and left sides of your body. These mark the upper boundary of your core.
4. Now that you've made a "touch memory" of these four points, imagine connecting them with lines to form a square that encircles your body. This is your core; the location of your psoas muscles and ventral vagal nerve system.
5. Take a deep breath and concentrate on drawing air directly into the middle of this square while allowing it to expand.
6. As you breathe out, relax all of the muscles within the square. Repeat this several times until the muscles of your core are completely relaxed.

Once you become adept at interoception, you'll be able to practice this relaxation method while sitting or standing as part of your daily regimen of self-regulation.

Method 2: Soft Palate Relaxation

Here, your goal is to locate and then relax the muscles of your soft palate.

1. Sit down comfortably and shift your focus to the muscles along the roof of your mouth.
2. Release all the tension in this area.
3. Now expand your focus to include the muscles in your face and jaw.
4. Release the tension in these muscles too.
5. Next, with all of these muscles relaxed, silently say the letter "R" to yourself and try to gently maintain the subtle arch this creates in the roof of your mouth for five seconds.
6. Repeat this exercise five times.
7. Notice the relaxation in your body

Method 3: Diaphragmatic or "Belly" Breathing

Diaphragmatic breathing offers another proven way to rapidly restore us to PNS dominance. Here's the four-step method recommended by the Cleveland Clinic.

1. Sit comfortably, with your knees bent and your shoulders, head, and neck relaxed.

2. Locate your diaphragm by placing one hand below your rib cage and the other on your upper chest. As you breathe, you will feel your diaphragm rising and falling.
3. Breathe in slowly through your nose so that your stomach moves outwards against your hand. Count in your head and make sure the inward breath lasts at least five seconds. Pay attention to the feeling of the air filling your lungs. The hand on your chest should remain as still as possible.
4. Tighten your stomach muscles, letting them fall inward as you exhale through pursed lips. The hand on your upper chest must remain as still as possible.
5. Repeat steps 1–4 five times.
6. Notice the relaxation in your body

Method 4: Shifting Focus to Your Peripheral Vision

This method was originally developed by the U.S. military to train snipers. Fortunately, it works just as well for civilians.

1. Find a spot at eye level that's located 5–10 feet in front of you.
2. Focus your eyes for five seconds on that spot.
3. Now soften your focus until the spot becomes blurry. Hold that for five seconds.
4. Still facing forward and without moving your eyes, shift your focus to your peripheral vision. Do this simultaneously with both eyes.

5. Maintain your peripheral focus for 10 seconds.
6. Repeat steps 1–5 five times.
7. Notice the relaxation in your body.

[Optional] If you're having difficulty shifting your focus from the center to the periphery, try extending your arms in front of you at an angle of roughly 75–80 degrees to your face. Now, when it's time to shift to your peripheral vision, wiggle your fingers to help you find the periphery. Make sure to keep your eyes facing forward while you do so.

WORKSHEET 2:

Self-Regulation Practice

It's time to start practicing the skill of self-regulation in the real world. At this point, you should already have chosen the relaxation method or methods that work best for you. For the next three days, perform self-regulation 5–10 times a day as you go about your normal routine. On each occasion, use the worksheet below to note down the level of tension you're feeling before and after self-regulating, which muscles were involved, and the method you used to invoke the relaxation response. We'll revisit this worksheet in Chapter 5, when you craft your covenant and code of honor, and again in Chapter 6, when we identify your triggers and establish your stress baseline.

Date	**Time**	**Muscle Tension** (1 = no tension to 5 = high)	**Tension Location** (Which muscles were tense)	**Relaxation Method** (The one you used)	**Results** (How you felt afterwards)

Date	Time	**Muscle Tension** (1 = no tension to 5 = high)	**Tension Location** (Which muscles were tense)	**Relaxation Method** (The one you used)	**Results** (How you felt afterwards)

Date	**Time**	**Muscle Tension** (1 = no tension to 5 = high)	**Tension Location** (Which muscles were tense)	**Relaxation Method** (The one you used)	**Results** (How you felt after-wards)

CHAPTER 5

Intentionality: The Key to a Productive and Satisfying Life

> *"One's only rival is one's own potentialities. One's only failure is failing to live up to one's own possibilities."*
>
> — ABRAHAM MASLOW —

Every morning, I wake up and make the same solemn resolution. Today, unlike every other day, I will succeed in my quest to be the perfect instrument of love and peace on this planet. I will treat everyone I encounter with unflagging kindness and compassion. I will *not* lose control and strike back. Then, somehow, my good intentions fly out the window as soon as I slide behind the wheel of my car and venture out into the snarling traffic of the busy highway.

Chronic stress and trauma do much more than damage our bodies and minds through dysregulation. They also carve deep spiritual and moral wounds by shattering the essential, largely unstated assumptions about ourselves and the world around us that imbue our lives with meaning and purpose. Instead of viewing the world as a fundamentally benevolent place, where right action reaps rewards and wrong actions are punished, we perceive it as hostile and capricious. Instead of feeling empowered, optimistic, and free, we perceive ourselves as helpless victims. Ultimately, we lose every vestige of the hope and conviction of self-efficacy we all need to feel joy, connect with others, and pursue our passions and dreams.

The damage is compounded when we lose control and act out, cursing a fellow motorist, exploding at a co-worker, or screaming at a loved one. How are we to make sense of our values if we abrogate them every time we're overwhelmed by stress? How can we know or trust ourselves if we chronically breach our integrity by acting in ways that contradict our core beliefs? In psychological terms, how do we shift from an external locus of control to an internal one that empowers us to live in accordance with our morals and ethics?

In short, how do we move beyond our chronic entrenched reactivity to live truly intentional lives?

A Formula for Hope

Forward-Facing Trauma Therapy provides an answer. It offers a moral antidote to chronic stress and dysregulation that is deceptively simple but profound in its implications. To heal ourselves, we must make intentional use of the "space" Viktor Frankl described that lies between stimulus and response. In that space, with a relaxed body and clarity of mind, we can consult our moral compass and allow the best within us to guide our actions. Like self-regulation, the recipe for intentional living is simple but not easy. It takes practice and perseverance. But the effort is well worth it, because the resulting effects are immediate, enduring, and transformational. I believe this capacity—the ability to live with fidelity to our principles—is the state Maslow refers to at the apex of his famous pyramid. Living intentionally *is* self-actualization.

Every time we succeed in acting intentionally, we grow stronger and more resilient. Our moral wounds heal bit by bit as the hypervigilance of SNS dominance gives way to the relaxed awareness of a regulated nervous system. Our fractured "spiritual skeleton" begins to mend itself organically, and the destructive symptoms of stress and its aftermath lose their grip upon us. We begin to feel lighter and more optimistic. Small successes lead to greater, more far-reaching ones as this process evolves into a deep satisfaction with ourselves and our lives.

The people in our lives sense the tectonic shift taking place inside us and begin to treat us in new ways that reinforce the positive changes we're making as we evolve and grow. Our virtuous circle expands, building strength upon strength. As we learn to trust ourselves, we become increasingly confident, less reactive, and more capable of love and intimacy. As our relationships improve, our social engagement system kicks in more frequently, soothing us when we're triggered and further enhancing our resilience. Gradually and inevitably, our psyche and soul align to make us whole again.

When we apply Forward-Facing Trauma Therapy, we become the midwives of our own rebirth. We become empowered and inspired to transform ourselves into the people we always wanted to be, living intentional lives replete with hope, meaning, and a noble purpose.

Getting Started

For more than 2,000 years, navigators traversed the seas with assurance by taking a fix from Polaris or the North Star to determine their location and the direction home. Without this celestial reference point, they might have been lost forever. In much the same way, we must orient ourselves to our own "moral true north" if we hope to successfully navigate the shoals of everyday life. Thus, in Forward-Facing Trauma Therapy, we always begin our journey to intentionality by embarking upon a discernment process to identify our core values, mission, and beliefs.

Some of us may already have embraced a fully constructed moral framework that was passed down to us from our parents, teachers, or spiritual leaders. Others may have lost faith in their moral training or possess only vague intuitions of who they are or want to be. Still others may have been so deeply wounded that they have embraced nihilism, rejecting all religious and moral principles entirely and adopting the cynical view that nothing, least of all our own behavior, has any real meaning or significance. Regardless, this fundamental quest for our "true north" principles is essential because it forces us to identify our often unspoken and unacknowledged moral assumptions, state them explicitly, and then align our behavior accordingly. In FFTT, we complete this process of discernment and self-discovery by crafting three documents:

1. Your **mission statement** defines what you believe to be your purpose as a human being living on this planet. Why are you here? What unique talents and perspectives do you bring to this life? What would make your life

truly worthwhile, not only for yourself but also for those around you?

2. Your **vision statement** describes the outcome and payoff of your efforts to heal and grow. When you fulfill your mission, what will have changed in your life? Who will you be? What will you be doing personally, professionally, and spiritually? Your vision statement must be so vivid and compelling that it energizes and sustains you throughout the arduous process of practicing ongoing self-regulation and intentionality in your daily life.

3. Your **code of honor** articulates the fundamental moral and ethical principles that will guide your behavior from this point forward, particularly when you're triggered. What constitutes right action? How should you choose between two actions when they appear to be morally equivalent? Your code of honor banishes all ambiguity and rationalizations, delineating clear guidelines for you to follow as you make sense of the world and your place within it.

Collectively, these three documents comprise the "moral compass" that will guide you on your journey to intentional living. Consider the metaphor of a train, with your vision statement defining your destination, your mission statement constituting the engine and cars, and your code of honor furnishing the tracks upon which the train is traveling. The longer you remain on track without derailing, the more quickly and easily you'll achieve your vision.

It's time now to start crafting your own vision statement, mission statement, and code of honor by completing the three exercises below. Don't overthink this process or try to produce perfect prose. What's most important is to be honest with yourself and to let the exercises guide you through the deeply personal process of self-exploration and self-definition. Don't be surprised if you find yourself changing or elaborating upon what you've written as time goes on. These documents tend to be organic and evolve in much the same way we do. The changing nature of our moral compass is a sure sign that we're making meaningful progress toward becoming the fully-realized person we choose to be rather than someone whose life has been disfigured by the wounds of our past.

At some point, you may feel confident enough to share these documents with others so they can support you in your journey and help you get back on track when you veer into dysregulation. For now, though, they're for your eyes only.

Exercise 1: Crafting Your Vision Statement

Close your eyes and picture yourself attending your own retirement party. As you sit on the dais, each attendee stands up in turn to give a short speech honoring you for having achieved your vision. What is each guest saying about you? What qualities or accomplishments are they praising you for? Jot down some notes to refer to as you begin crafting your vision statement.

Suggestions:

1. Your vision statement should consist of 2–5 sentences written in the present tense. For example, write "I am financially secure" rather than "I will achieve financial security."

2. State an overarching objective rather than a specific one. For example, write "I am a national leader in the field of financial planning" rather than "I have 450 active clients."
3. Write in the first person (e.g., "I am a successful and respected corporate attorney.").
4. Make sure your vision statement is compelling enough to keep you motivated and inspired when you encounter setbacks.
5. Remember, you are writing a vision for yourself, not for your spouse, parents, children, boss, or anyone else. This is the time to think deeply about what you want out of life.
6. Be bold. Don't limit your vision to what you could accomplish now. Consider who you could become and what that person could accomplish if they no longer experienced fear and stress. Reach for the stars.

Most importantly, have fun and recognize there is no "wrong" way to write a vision statement. Okay, let's start writing!

My Vision Statement

EXERCISE 2:

Crafting Your Mission Statement

In this exercise, your goal is nothing short of defining your mission in life. Why are you here? What is your "best self"—the person you could become if the shackles of fear, anger, and stress were forever banished from your life? How would you fully express your talents and creativity? What role would you play in helping others become their best selves?

Preparation: Part 1

There are two parts to this exercise. Part 1 consists of five questions. Try to come up with at least five good answers for each one. Keep them short and concise, spending no more than a total of 15 minutes on Part 1.

1. Why are you alive? What is your purpose for living on this planet?

____

____

____

____

____

____

2. What do you want to be when you grow up?

3. What dreams do you have for yourself that are, as yet, unfulfilled?

4. What is REALLY important to you?

5. What are your greatest strengths?

Read back over what you've just written and then circle the 3–5 responses you feel are most accurate and meaningful to you. What do they tell you about yourself? How well does your current life match up with the mission you'd formulate for yourself if your life was stress-free? Take a few minutes now to note down your impressions about this remarkable person you're learning about, perhaps for the very first time.

Preparation: Part 2

Next, spend one minute on each of the 10 "fill-in" sentence fragments below to begin articulating the key elements of your mission statement.

It is my mission:

To live:

____

____

____

____

____

____

To work:

____

____

____

____

____

____

To continue:

To love:

To be:

To become:

To believe:

To promote:

To strive:

To seek:

Now, read over everything you wrote in Parts 1 and 2. Using these new insights, write your mission statement on the following page.

My Mission Statement

Exercise 3: Crafting Your Code of Honor

This exercise will help you establish the moral foundation of an intentional, principle-based life. Your goal is to identify the ethical guidelines you'll be applying in the course of pursuing your mission and achieving your vision.

Preparation

Start by choosing 10–12 words from the list on the next page that most accurately reflect your moral and ethical convictions. Then, write a declarative sentence for each one that states your aspiration to abide by these rules without fail. If honesty is important to you, for example, you might write "I am always honest with myself and others." Of course, as fallible human beings, none of us can adhere to our morals and ethics as fully and faithfully as we might wish. But, for now, our goal is to set as high a bar as possible for our future behavior. Over time, as we continue to practice self-regulation, our code of honor and modes of behavior will increasingly converge until we are consistently living in accordance with our deepest beliefs.

My Principles

A leader	Active	Approach vs. Avoidance
Assertive	Challenging	Commitment
Compassionate	Conservative	Courageous
Creative	Detailed	Effective
Efficient	Ethical	Facilitative
Faithful	Farsighted	Fearless
Frugal	Greedy	Honest
Hopeful	Humorous	Joyful
Just	Liberal	Loving
Moderate	Optimistic	Outspoken
Parenting	Passionate	Peaceable
Powerful	Productive	Resilient
Responsible	Scientific	Secure
Self-confident	Service	Strong
Tolerant	Truthful	

My Code of Honor

The Rewards of Intentional Living

As we've seen, the biology of the stress response, our attitudes about life, and our behavior toward others are inextricably linked. Every time we breach our integrity, we reopen the moral wounds caused by trauma and chronic stress, reinforcing our dysregulation and consigning ourselves to a life bereft of meaning and self-efficacy. However, the reverse is also true. Each time we act in accordance with our moral precepts, we take a significant step toward healing our moral wounds and knitting together the shards of our shattered "spiritual skeletons."

From this

Figure 10A: Reactivity

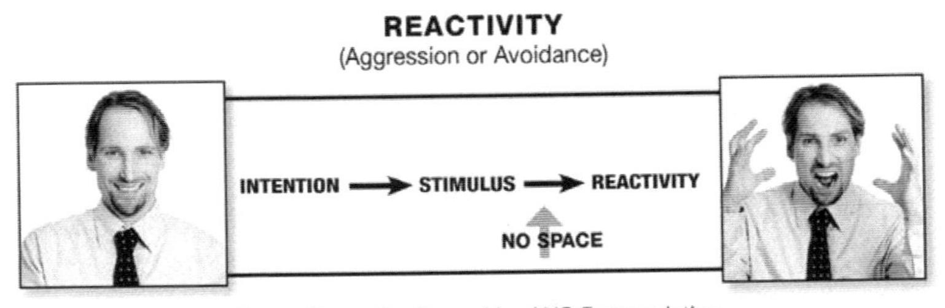

to this

Figure 10B: Intentionality

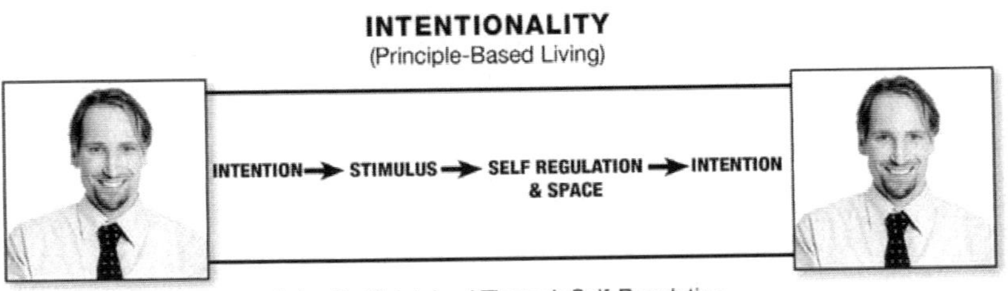

The more we live in harmony with our true and honest selves, the more people around us will respond in kind, sustaining us in our journey and reinforcing our sense of personal worth and self-efficacy. Yet the entire process remains entirely within our own control, fully empowering us every step of the way.

Like interoception and self-regulation, the recipe for acting with intentionality is simple but not easy. Sometimes, you'll be so overwhelmed by the destructive effects of stress and trauma that you'll experience a setback. You'll act out and feel you've let yourself down. Don't believe it. The process of acquiring intentionality is like that of a baby learning to walk. We all fall down sometimes. But every time we get back on our feet and "walk the intentional walk," our balance improves and our steps become surer. We begin to achieve the moral and spiritual rebirth that is the singular goal of Forward-Facing Trauma Therapy.

Of course, every journey has missteps. In the next chapter, we'll learn how to identify and manage the triggers that propel us into dysregulation. We'll see how the resulting breaches of our integrity provide us with essential opportunities to grow rather than excuses for indulging in guilt and self-pity. By learning to identify and tolerate these missteps while they're occurring in real-time, we'll begin to develop the durable insights and perspectives we need to live with intention.

For now, however, you've taken the essential first steps toward achieving wholeness, integrity, authenticity, and intentionality. Armed with your vision statement, mission statement, and code of honor, you have all of the tools you need to begin tapping into your unique gifts and realizing your full potential. Now it's time to start applying your newfound direction, purpose, and motivation to your everyday life. You'll be amazed at what you can achieve when you evolve into the person you were always meant to be.

CHAPTER 6

Identifying Your Triggers and Establishing Your Stress Baseline

"The journey is the thing."

—HOMER —

In the preceding chapters, we examined the biological and evolutionary basis for the stress response and considered the difference between episodic "good stress," which helps us perform at our best, and pervasive "bad stress," which can send our threat-response systems into overdrive. We saw how chronic dysregulation can cause us to breach our integrity and behave in ways that undermine our essential sense of dignity and self-efficacy.

Next, we learned about self-regulation and why it's so effective in creating the "precious space" that is the prerequisite for making intentional choices. We completed a discernment process in which we identified our core beliefs and codified the overarching moral and ethical framework we need to guide our actions during these moments of clarity. Our final step is to identify the real-world "triggers" that plunge us into dysregulation and then to begin applying self-regulation and intentionality to rob them of their destructive power. In short, we're ready to begin the day-to-day process of transforming our lives and becoming the mature, self-actualized individuals we were always meant to be.

What Is a Trigger?

It's helpful to begin by considering what a trigger is *not*. Consider these three scenarios:

- An aggressive driver veers in front of you and cuts you off.
- Your boss emails you that it's time for your annual performance review.
- A little girl throws a tantrum and blocks your cart at your local supermarket, as her mother looks on without intervening.

As humans, we're always looking for ways to make sense of our surroundings in order to meet our basic needs for safety, security, and acceptance. As a result, we're likely to attribute hostile motives to the aggressive driver in order to justify our own aggressive response. Or, like Joshua, we may start imagining our boss firing us and feel a mounting sense of anxiety and dread as the meeting approaches. Or we might feel contempt for the mother for failing to control her errant child. Yet, in all three cases, what we're *really* doing is shifting to an external locus of control in which we attribute our stress response to the environment around us rather than recognizing that our reactions reside entirely within our own bodies and minds.

External events don't cause these visceral reactions. They simply provide the sensory information our threat-response systems use to assess danger. Therefore, a trigger is best understood as a form of sensory information that our threat-response system has interpreted as a sign of imminent danger. Let me say this in a slightly different way. *A trigger is nothing more than a sound, a smell, or some other form of sensory input that our threat-response system associates—however tangentially—with our experiences of past painful learning.* And, as we've seen, when our threat-response systems are thrown into dysregulation, our ability to accurately perceive threats is severely compromised.

Thus, a combat veteran contending with PTSD may react to a sudden loud noise they associate with an IED explosion with what appears to be an exaggerated startle response. Yet, their response is entirely appropriate when you consider the conditions under which the association of noise to truly life-threatening danger first occurred. Likewise, the anxiety and dread we feel at the prospect of our annual review may seem utterly out of proportion until we recognize that we've been triggered into re-experiencing some painful or traumatic experience from our past. The duration and intensity of our stress response will vary in accordance with the extent and power of this past painful learning. But, no matter where we stand on the stress continuum, the underlying stress response mechanisms are always the same.

The Contributions of Forward-Facing Trauma Therapy

One of the most crucial contributions of Forward-Facing Trauma Therapy is the core insight that *we do not need to excavate the past to eliminate triggers and forever free ourselves from the insidious effects of stress.* Instead, we can simply learn to *recognize* when we've been triggered and then *respond* by relaxing our bodies. Every time we apply self-regulation in this way, we invoke the biological process of desensitization through reciprocal inhibition that we first described in Chapter 4. Gradually and inevitably, the frequency, intensity, and duration of our stress responses are reduced. We no longer feel controlled by forces outside ourselves. We no longer perceive danger where it doesn't exist.

This process might prove overwhelmingly difficult if it required us to evaluate every sensory impression we experience on a moment-to-moment basis as a potential trigger. Fortunately, FFTT makes this process remarkably simple. Employing our newfound skill of interoception, we can scan our bodies every few minutes to sense whether we're tensing the muscles in any of our stress hot spots. If we detect muscle tension, we can correctly conclude that we've recently been triggered and take this as our cue to invoke the relaxation response.

To accelerate this re-regulation process, it's helpful to start identifying the kinds of people and situations that have triggered us in the past. This enables us to oppose triggers before they can fully energize our stress response, or better yet, to use self-regulation proactively to prevent them from engaging at all. This is the process we'll explore in the exercises below.

Of course, our goal in Forward-Facing Trauma Therapy is more ambitious than the simple elimination of stress from our lives. We're aiming at nothing short of personal transformation; restarting the natural maturational processes that have been stalled by our reflexive reactivity. This means developing new, more adaptive strategies for responding to stress that preserve our personal integrity and align with our moral compass. In

FFTT, we rely on the wisdom of our bodies and psyches, not our conscious minds, to begin guiding us toward wholeness.

The ongoing practice of FFTT continually moves us closer to living our best lives inside of our best selves. Aristotle captured this ideal with the Greek word *eudaemonia*, which refers to the happy state in which we experience a life of "activity governed by reason." While eudaemonia is synonymous with happiness, there is a nuanced difference. Eudaemonia cannot be achieved through pleasure-seeking and consumerism. It requires a disciplined process of pursuing and consistently achieving excellence in one's life. Forward-Facing Trauma Therapy helps us achieve this goal by removing the internal barriers that prevent us from fully expressing our inborn talents and capabilities. In a very real sense, FFTT can be seen as a step-by-step process for achieving eudaemonia in our daily lives.

What Are Your Triggers?

Around 500 BC, the great Chinese philosopher Confucius wrote, "No matter where you go, there you are." These words of wisdom are just as relevant today as they were during the sage's lifetime. Whether we're at work, at home, or at play, we carry our triggers with us; projecting them onto the people and situations around us and then reacting in ways that breach our integrity.

In Exercises 1 and 2, we'll consider the impact your triggers may be having at work and at home. Once you feel comfortable with these exercises, you can start applying them more broadly to every sphere of your life.

Exercise 1: Mapping Your Breaches to Triggers

Over the next five days, use Worksheet 1 below to write down five occasions in which you breached the moral compass you crafted in Chapter 5. Our goal here is to identify the triggers that are most severely degrading your performance and compromising your integrity.

In column 1: Note down the date and time the breach occurred. You may discover that there are certain times of the day in which you're most likely to become overwhelmed by stress.

In column 2: Note down where you were when the breach occurred. For example, "I was in a meeting with my manager to review my progress on a current project" or "I was in the bedroom getting ready to go out to dinner with my spouse."

In column 3: Note down the details of the breach. A short description will do. For example, "I blamed a co-worker for failing to give me the information I needed in time to meet my deadline" or "I complained to my wife that she was not getting ready fast enough."

In column 4: Note down what happened one to five minutes before your breach. What were you thinking and feeling? For example, "I became anxious recalling past occasions when I felt my boss had treated me unfairly" or "I started thinking about how much I disliked the hosts of the dinner party we'd be attending."

In column 5: Note down the stress "hot spot" in your body where you felt the most muscle tension after being triggered. This will be the focus of your self-regulation efforts when you move on to Exercise 2.

In column 6: The "Stress Thermometer" in Figure 11 utilizes a modified version of the Subjective Units of Distress Scale (SUDS) scale developed by Joseph Wolpe[12] to benchmark the efficacy of his systematic desensitization approach to treating South African soldiers suffering from what was then called "war neurosis." Use this SUDS scale to rate the level of distress you felt after being triggered, with zero indicating no distress at all and 10 indicating the most distress you can ever imagine feeling.

Figure 11: Stress Thermometer

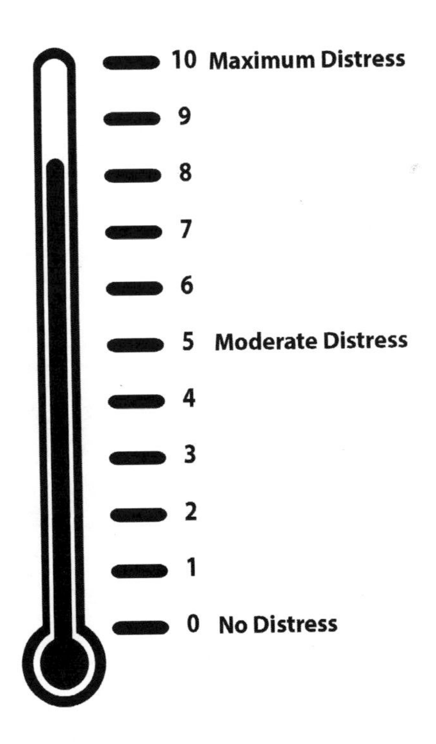

When the week is over, take a careful look at this "trigger/breach diary" and see if you can't find some revealing patterns emerging. For example, you may find that at work:

- "Whenever my boss asks to see me, I start feeling anxious and tense up my neck and shoulders because I think I'm about to be criticized. When that happens, I become defensive and refuse to accept suggestions on improving my work."
- "In meetings, I often feel like everyone else has better ideas than I do. I tense my lips and jaw and have trouble thinking of anything to say. If I'm called upon, I simply agree with whatever everyone else has been saying and offer no ideas of my own."
- "When clients call me with problems, I sometimes lie or blame others. For example, I denied receiving a purchase order I had actually misplaced because I was afraid I would get into trouble."

Or that at home:

- "When I have to socialize with people I don't know that well, I feel anxious and my neck and shoulders get tight. When that happens, I tend to take it out on my wife and get critical or defensive with her."
- "At home, I often feel like my family is ganging up on me. When that happens, I feel upset, my jaw and lips tighten up, and I need a drink to calm myself down."
- "When my wife asks me to wash the dishes or take out the garbage, I feel as if I'm a little kid being ordered around by my mother. When that happens, I grit my

teeth and complete the chore as quickly and sloppily as possible, 'accidentally' breaking dishes or slamming the garbage cover down as loudly as I can."

WORKSHEET 1: MAPPING YOUR BREACHES TO TRIGGERS

Date/ Time	Setting	Breach	Trigger	Hot Spot	SUDS Score

Exercise 2: Planning for Intentionality

Achieving intentionality requires much more from us than simply deciding how *not* to behave when we're triggered. We also need a set of principle-based behaviors to guide us after we have self-regulated. In FFTT, we refer to this as having "intention in mind." Therefore, in this exercise, you'll apply your moral compass to each of the breaches you listed in Exercise 1 and then identify new responses that preserve your integrity. Begin by choosing three to five of the most powerful trigger/breach combinations from Worksheet 1 and entering them into columns 1 and 2 below. Now, in each case, enter your new "intention in mind" behaviors in column 3. Later, in Exercise 3, you'll start enacting your intentionality and tracking the resulting improvements in your levels of stress and sense of personal integrity.

Worksheet 2: Remapping Our Behavior

Trigger	Prior "Breach Response"	New "Intentional Response"

Exercise 3: Applying Your Intentionality

You've been honest and forthright in identifying your triggers and their pernicious effects on your personal integrity. You've defined clear and actionable "intention in mind" behaviors to guide you when you do get triggered. The person who completed these exercises may be new to you. But he or she is fully deserving of your respect and admiration. Take a moment to congratulate yourself for demonstrating your sincere commitment to becoming your best self. Now it's time to "walk the talk" by applying intentionality to your real-world experiences.

Begin by sharing everything you've learned about yourself with someone important in your life. Let's call this person your "accountability partner." Tell them about your goals for eliminating your reactivity and ask for their support in helping you live up to your ideals. Their support and encouragement will go a long way toward helping you stay on track when you inevitably fall short, as we all do from time to time.

Now, over the next five days, use Worksheets 3 and 4 to write down five situations in which you applied your "intention in mind" behaviors instead of breaching your integrity.

In column 1: Note down instances in which you experienced a trigger that previously caused you to breach your integrity.

In column 2: Note down the level of distress you felt prior to self-regulating, using our modified SUDS scale.

In column 3: Note down the self-regulation strategy you applied (e.g., relaxing your core, etc.).

In column 4: Note down the intentional behavior you enacted after self-regulating.

In column 5: Note down your modified SUDS score AFTER behaving intentionally.

In column 6: Calculate the reduction in your level of stress by subtracting column 2 from column 5.

WORKSHEET 3: TRACKING YOUR INTENTIONALITY IN THE WORKPLACE

Trigger	Starting SUDS	Self-Regulation Strategy	Intentional Behavior	Ending SUDS	Stress Reduction

Worksheet 4: Tracking Your Intentionality at Home

Trigger	Starting SUDS	Self-Regulation Strategy	Intentional Behavior	Ending SUDS	Stress Reduction

Exercise 4: Sustaining Your Intentionality

At the end of five days, read over what you've written and consider how far you've come. Did you amaze your colleagues with your brilliant ideas during a meeting? Did your wife or husband give you a hug and say you've become the perfect spouse? Probably not. But at work, you may have been able to enhance and expand on someone else's ideas when you would have previously sat silent and resentful. At home, you may have avoided fighting over some trivial disagreement and incrementally improved one of your most treasured relationships in the process.

Acting intentionally will not optimize your performance or help you achieve perfection overnight. But, if you stay the course, you'll find yourself spending more and more time in the sweet spot of the Yerkes-Dodson curve, where you're consistently operating within your optimal energy zone and behaving in accordance with your personal integrity.

Consider the sharp reductions in stress you've achieved simply by confronting your triggers with a relaxed body and intentional behaviors. Now, consider the amazing gains you could achieve over the coming months and years by applying these same strategies to every triggering experience in your life.

In the space below, reflect on what you've learned over the course of reading this book. How did you feel about yourself and your future before you started on your road to intentional living? How do you feel now? Write down your thoughts about applying your newfound skills even more broadly in your personal and professional lives and jot down some initial plans for getting started.

Once you master the skills of self-regulation and intentional living, personal transformation truly is within your grasp. You are well on your way to becoming your best self!

My Journey to an Intentional Life

CHAPTER 7

Four Stories of Personal Transformation

"One can choose to go back toward safety or forward toward growth. Growth must be chosen again and again; fear must be overcome again and again."

— ABRAHAM MASLOW —

As we've seen, Forward-Facing Trauma Therapy is much more than simply a biologically informed methodology for eliminating stress. It's the foundation for a life in which you are empowered to continue growing, connecting with others, and living in accordance with your most deeply held beliefs and aspirations. It provides tools that anyone, at any point in their lives, can acquire and master with a little time and effort. It truly is never too late to begin living a stress-free, intentional life.

Over the decades, I've worked with thousands of clients from all walks of life. I'm always inspired and profoundly moved when I witness the amazing transformations that are possible when these individuals free themselves of their entrenched reactivity. I'd like to share the stories of four of these remarkable women and men with you now, along with the "tools for hope" they employed in our work together. Here, then, are the stories of Jennifer, Gene, Alysia, and Clyde.

Jennifer's Journey

"Jennifer" is a 36-year-old stay-at-home mom from an affluent Dallas suburb. She and her husband of 12 years, "Jim," have two sons, "Billy" (age 9) and "Andy" (age 7).

When Jennifer first arrived at my office, I was immediately struck by her downcast demeanor, her avoidance of eye contact, and the flat tone of voice she used to explain her reason for entering therapy. "I'm a terrible mother," she told me. Both of her boys had been diagnosed with ADHD, and their disruptive behavior at school was now reaching critical proportions. She and her husband had recently been summoned to the principal's office, where they were warned that both boys were likely to be left back unless their grades and behavior improved dramatically. They left the meeting feeling frightened and humiliated.

Jennifer was at her wit's end. She had tried "everything" to make her boys behave, including various forms of punishments and rewards. But none of these strategies had proven effective for very long. At this point, she was so angry and exasperated that she found herself flying off the handle at even the smallest provocations. With evident shame, she related a recent episode in which she lost control and swept the family's dinner dishes onto the floor after Billy and Andy started throwing food at each other.

Jennifer's unhappiness was compounded by Jim's claim that it was her job to "make things work with the kids," a role she was clearly failing to perform to his satisfaction. He felt no compunction about expressing these sentiments in front of the kids. Billy had even taken to repeating some of his father's pet criticisms to bait her. Jim's constant carping was taking its toll, and the couple's relationship had deteriorated to the point where they were barely speaking to each other. Both of their children had noticed and were starting to comment on the conflict between them. "I just want to run away from it all," Jennifer told me.

Although she ascribed these feelings to her "failures" as a mother, I suspected they might have a deeper origin. In college, Jennifer had been diagnosed with major depressive disorder by a psychiatrist who had prescribed Prozac, an SSRI (selective serotonin reuptake inhibitor) drug that can sometimes be helpful in alleviating symptoms of depression. Prozac did provide Jennifer with some relief, but she also experienced several unpleasant side effects, including a weight gain of 10–15 pounds that she found particularly distasteful. Consequently, Jennifer would invariably stop taking her pills as soon as she started feeling better, only to see her symptoms return a few months later. In truth, chronic depression and feelings of sadness and self-hatred had dogged Jennifer throughout most of her life, and she had experienced a serious episode of postpartum depression after the birth of her second son, Andy.

As we delved further into her past, Jennifer described a stern and rigid father, who ruled the family home with an iron fist, and a passive, well-meaning mother, who was loving toward Jennifer but primarily concerned with "keeping the peace." This was a worthy goal given her husband's tendency to fly into sudden rages in which he would slap her across the face and reduce her to tears. Jennifer witnessed episodes like these with some regularity throughout much of her childhood and adolescence.

As a result, she was careful to follow all of her father's rules. However, being a "model child" didn't protect Jennifer from his sarcastic comments about her looks, manner of dress, and choice of friends, critiques that she found especially wounding during her teen years. I couldn't help noticing some striking similarities between Jennifer's father and her husband, Jim, although she herself didn't seem aware of the obvious parallels. It was clear to me that Jennifer had been contending with chronic stress for many years and that treating the resulting dysregulation would be a key focus of our work together.

I concluded our first session together by carefully explaining the goals and methods of Forward-Facing Trauma Therapy. I emphasized the sense of empowerment that comes with recognizing that we can free ourselves of stress once we reregulate our underlying threat-response systems. I then described the "simple but not easy" self-regulation techniques we would be employing and the profound satisfaction that comes with intentional living. Jennifer seemed somewhat dubious, but agreed "for the sake of my family" to work on the first homework assignment I gave her: to write a vision statement and bring it with her to our next session.

When she returned a week later, Jennifer described the difficulty she had encountered in drafting her vision statement. "All I could focus on was becoming the kind of mother who knows how to raise well-behaved, well-adjusted children," she explained. As the session progressed, however, Jennifer was able to expand her vision to encompass her own needs for a satisfying family life. By the time we ended that day, Jennifer's vision statement read, "I am enjoying the company of my husband and children in a home filled with love and laughter."

With her vision now firmly in place, Jennifer was ready to formulate her mission statement, "To live fully, caring for myself as well as caring for my family," and her code of honor, "I am self-confident and assertive with my husband, friends, and children."

After trying out several different relaxation techniques, Jennifer chose diaphragmatic breathing as her preferred method of self-regulation and practiced it assiduously between sessions. She also came to understand and accept the fact that her influence over her children was limited and, therefore, that her belief she was solely responsible for their misbehavior was misplaced. The only person she could ever hope to control, I explained, was herself.

In our fourth session, we focused on identifying the triggers that were evoking Jennifer's amped-up stress response, which I believed to be the root cause of her depression and the source of the shame that she so often experienced as a wife and mother. We also examined the ways in which these stress responses "turned off" her higher brain functions and caused her to breach her integrity. Unsurprisingly, the sound of Jim's voice haranguing her proved to be one of her most potent triggers, a perceived threat she articulated as, "My husband is going to leave me. I'll never be good enough. I'm unlovable."

Now, we were ready to identify a new set of behaviors that Jennifer could draw upon whenever her newfound skills of self-regulation enabled her to create the "precious space" needed to act intentionally. "From now on," she resolved, "whenever I'm triggered by my husband or sons, I'll either respond assertively or choose not to engage until I'm no longer feeling stressed."

Armed with her new tools for self-regulation and intentionality, Jennifer began to develop fresh insights about herself and the chronic stress that had shaped her. Gradually, she came to recognize how the visceral sense of fear and shame she had felt witnessing her mother's degradation was identical to the rage and self-loathing that were now being provoked by her husband's sarcasm and personal attacks. This burgeoning self-awareness helped her to distinguish between situations in which Jim was being hypercritical like her father and those in which he was expressing, however disproportionately, his genuine concerns about their two sons.

Jennifer's growing sense of self-mastery also afforded her enough self-confidence to ignore some of Jim's criticisms and to correctly interpret them as manifestations of his own unregulated stress response. As she became less reactive and more empathetic, Jim calmed down too. He became less critical and more willing to acknowledge their shared responsibility for disciplining their sons. Slowly and incrementally, their relationship began to improve.

Thanks to her newfound poise and self-possession, Jennifer was able to model for her sons a more constructive way of communicating her concerns and enforcing house rules. To her surprise and pleasure, Billy and Andy began to emulate her calm demeanor and more modulated responses. Although they were still far from "perfect," her sons' behavior improved markedly and Billy stopped "sassing" her.

Now that Jennifer no longer perceived her sons' misbehavior as a personal failure (i.e., "threat"), she became less defensive and more relaxed. She manifested her growing sense of self-worth by reaching out to other mothers at her sons' school, learning in the process that she was far from unique in finding parenthood both difficult and unrewarding at times. As she stopped judging herself so harshly, she became more open and receptive to others. Her sense of shame and isolation diminished and she began volunteering at school events and reinvigorating lapsed friendships. At school functions, she fell into conversation with other mothers and soon developed an extensive peer support network that proved to be an enduring source of comfort and connection.

With her family and social lives improving, Jennifer was ready to address the first part of her mission, "To live fully, caring for myself." She enrolled in an art class and joined a women's book club. During our last session together, Jennifer shared her plans to pursue a masters degree in accounting when her boys entered middle school. Jim, she noted with pleasure, supported this plan with a surprising degree of enthusiasm.

Today, Jennifer's life is more manageable than ever before, and the depression and shame that bedeviled her for so many years have finally lifted. Her boys still present challenges, and her life is far from perfect. But I'm confident that Jennifer is well on her way to becoming the fully realized person she was always meant to be.

Jennifer's Tools for Hope

- **Vision:** I'm enjoying the company of my husband and children in a home filled with love and laughter.
- **Mission Statement:** To live fully, caring for myself as well as caring for my family.
- **Code of Honor:** I'm self-confident and assertive with my husband, friends, and children.
- **Perceived Threat(s):**

  1. My husband is going to leave me.
  2. I'll never be good enough. I'm unlovable.

- **Trigger(s):** The sound of Jim's voice when he's criticizing me.
- **Intentional Behavior(s):** To respond assertively or choose not to engage until I'm no longer feeling stressed.

Gene's Journey

"Gene" is a 72-year-old retired widower who lives in a small town in upstate New York. A year earlier, his doctors had discovered a slow-growing inoperable brain tumor. According to his neurologist, the cancer was not life-threatening or likely to cause any noticeable cognitive deficits over the next three to five years. But Gene was not convinced. He lived in constant fear that the tumor's growth would accelerate, destroying his mind and reducing him to little more than a burden on his grown daughter and two sons until he finally succumbed to a horrible and ignominious death.

To prepare for the rapid decline he envisioned, Gene toured several assisted living facilities with his daughter in tow, steadfastly ignoring his doctor's opinion that he was years away from needing anything approaching this level of care. In fact, Gene was still quite active and independent. He was able to drive and kept busy volunteering at church events and participating in a weekly bridge club with a small group of friends. Still, he remained convinced that his life was over and often felt lonely and discouraged when he pondered his future. Most of all, Gene keenly missed his wife of 47 years, "Jeannie," who had died eight years earlier.

In the fall of 2013, Gene's children and pastor grew increasingly concerned when he began making dark statements about "knowing when it's your time" and "getting it over with" so "I can join my dear Jeannie in heaven." The only thing stopping him, they worried, was his deep faith in God and his conviction that suicide was a mortal sin.

That November, Gene's pastor suggested he consider talking with a professional about his growing despondency and referred him to my clinical practice. Gene, like many members of his generation, was convinced that "therapy is only for crazy people." So I was surprised and gratified when, at his pastor's insistence, Gene grudgingly agreed to meet with me.

From our opening moments together, Gene's deadpan sense of humor was very much in evidence. "There's nothing wrong with me except a little touch of brain cancer," he stated dryly when I asked what had brought him into therapy. I couldn't suppress a chuckle at this unexpected bit of gallows humor, which seemed to please him and break the ice.

Over the course of the next hour, Gene told me how much he missed Jeannie and expressed his belief that "only God can help me now." Still, he listened politely to my description of the methods and goals of Forward-Facing Trauma Therapy and—after much coaxing—agreed to return the following week with his vision statement.

As it turned out, Gene was unable to come up with either a vision or a mission statement. Believing that there was nothing meaningful left for him to do "here on this earth," he couldn't envision a future filled with anything other than illness, dependency, and death. However, he had no difficulty in defining his code of honor, which was deeply informed by his religious faith. So we took a different approach than I usually take with FFTT clients.

We began with his code of honor and worked backwards, imagining how someone who shared his values might spend their remaining years if they were not contending with cancer. Gene found this exercise both interesting and thought-provoking, although he remained unconvinced that it had any practical application to his own life. Still, it helped him to shift his focus from his own "doomed" future to one in which meaning might be derived from serving others.

However, the real turning point came during our third session, when I asked Gene, "Do you have the courage to live in accordance with God's plan for your remaining years? Do you want to truly live until you die?" This was something of a eureka moment for Gene. He was shocked into silence. Then, I saw a subtle change in his demeanor. His face cleared and he became very calm as he began to conceive of a future for himself that was guided exclusively by the precepts of his faith rather than by the inevitable consequences of aging and death.

Now, Gene was able to articulate a vision in which, "I'm vacationing with my family at the beach, where I'm playing with my granddaughter in the sand," as well as a mission "to be a loving grandfather and a source of comfort to other cancer survivors." For his code of honor, he wrote, "I am faithful and committed to my God and my family."

This provided the foundation we needed for Gene to develop his self-regulation skills and identify his most potent trigger: his monthly meetings with his oncologist. I suggested that Gene write down his vision, mission, and code of honor statements and bring them—along with photos of his extended family—to his next oncology appointment. Gene also decided to set aside time before and after the appointment for prayer and communion.

Both strategies proved to be effective, reducing his sense of dread and providing him with the confidence he needed to define several additional intentional behaviors. Chief among them was a plan to devote more of his time to his extended family, especially his grandchildren. Gene found their innocence and youthful exuberance a continuing source of delight and inspiration.

As the intensity of his fear and sadness abated, Gene began to explore additional ways to live with intentionality. He joined a cancer support group, where he shared his journey with other survivors and found comfort and acceptance that gave his own life new meaning and purpose. Grateful for these blessings, he also brought a new level of commitment to his church, where he became a shining example for others and an inspiration to his small community.

Gene's Tools for Hope

- **Vision:** I'm vacationing with my family at the beach, where I'm playing with my granddaughter in the sand.
- **Mission Statement:** To be a loving grandfather and a comfort to other cancer survivors.
- **Code of Honor:** I'm faithful and committed to my God and my family.
- **Perceived Threat(s):** I'm going to lose my mind and become a burden to my children.
- **Trigger(s):** Visiting the oncologist's office.
- **Intentional Behavior(s):**
  1. Staying grounded in the present by bringing photos

of my family and copies of my covenant and code of honor to my oncology appointments.

2. Spending time in prayer before and after my appointments.
3. Spending quality time with my extended family, especially my grandchildren.
4. Bringing comfort and support to other cancer survivors.

Alysia's Journey

"Alysia" was a 15-year-old high school student when I first met her. She was an only child who lived with her parents, "Hank" and "Charlotte," in an upper-middle-class neighborhood on the outskirts of Baltimore. Alysia had always been a well-behaved and studious child, able to amuse herself for hours on end writing imaginative poems and stories inspired by her two heroes, authors Suzanne Collins and J. K. Rowling.

Alysia's mother was not overly concerned when she found a handful of blood-soaked tissues wadded up at the bottom of Alysia's wastebasket while tidying up her room. However, she became alarmed several days later when she found one of Alysia's old T-shirts—stiff with dried blood—stuffed between her mattress and box spring, along with two blood-stained razor blades that Alysia had taken from her father's shaving kit.

When Hank and Charlotte confronted Alysia that evening, the teenager initially denied knowing anything about the T-shirt and razor blades. However, she finally confessed to having started cutting "a few weeks ago," insisting that "it's no big deal, lots of girls do it." Fearful that cutting might be a prelude to suicide and baffled by Alysia's dismissive attitude, Hank and Charlotte resolved to have her see a therapist. Alysia was referred to me a few days later.

I met first with Hank and Charlotte to get their perspectives on Alysia's cutting and to review her medical history. Although somewhat shy, they told me, Alysia had never seemed particularly unhappy or had any problems making friends. She had appeared to make a successful transition from the small middle school she previously attended to the more chaotic environment of the much larger high school where she was currently in her freshman year. Alysia had expressed some anxiety about her English teacher's policy to have students read their papers out loud in front of the class. But neither parent could imagine how this could lead to cutting and worried that it might be a harbinger of a serious mental illness.

Given what I had learned about Alysia so far, it seemed more likely to me that her cutting was an example of nonsuicidal self-injury (NSSI), a diagnostic category psychologists use to describe self-harming behaviors that are performed to self-soothe and manage anxiety rather than to cause life-threatening injuries or death. In recent years, NSSI has emerged as a serious and growing problem, particularly among adolescents. According to some studies, one-third to one-half of adolescents in the United States engage regularly in some form of self-injury behavior.[13] NSSI, I informed them, was particularly prevalent among girls aged 13 to 19, where as many as one in every 200 are thought to cut themselves on a regular basis.[14] Hank and Charlotte seemed somewhat relieved to hear that Alysia's cutting behavior was hardly unique and did not necessarily indicate a hitherto undetected mental illness.

When her parents returned to the waiting room, I asked Alysia to join me in my office for a private chat. Moments later, she stalked in, plopped down on the chair farthest away from mine and began pointedly ignoring me, staring out the window and fussing with her hair. This continued for some time. After a few attempts, however, I was finally able to get her talking. I made it clear that I had no intention of trying to force her to stop cutting. That would be up to her. But I did think it was important for us to understand her reasons for cutting and asked her to start keeping a journal. "Whenever you feel like cutting," I told her, "write down what's happening in your life and also how you feel before and after you cut." Reluctantly, she agreed.

During our next two sessions, Alysia described the intense anxiety she felt every time she was asked to stand up in English class to present her work and her fear that she would "mess up" and be humiliated. As we read her journal together, Alysia came to see how cutting relieved this anxiety and helped her feel more in control. This insight provided me with a useful context for explaining the biology of stress, how cutting evoked her relaxation response, and why cutting had proven so effective in reducing her anxiety, albeit temporarily. Fascinated in spite of herself, Alysia was now ready to begin Forward-Facing Trauma Therapy in earnest.

Alysia is one of those lucky people who possess an innate sense of who she is and what she wants to be. For her vision, she wrote, "I'm living in Paris writing my second novel." Her mission statement read, "I want to write books that open up new worlds for people." She also defined her code of honor as, "I'm creative and passionate in every aspect of my life."

Alysia had no difficulty in defining the perceived threat that was causing her anxiety or its most powerful trigger. For her perceived threat, Alysia wrote, "The other students will laugh and make fun of me. They'll see me as a loser." Her trigger was, "Any time I have to speak in front of a group of people, especially other students."

It was now time for Alysia to begin acquiring the self-regulation skills she would need to manage her stress more productively. She discovered that she could evoke her relaxation response using the progressive muscle relaxation and peripheral vision techniques I showed her. Our next task was to practice applying self-regulation whenever she was triggered.

Obviously, we weren't going to invite Alysia's classmates to a session so she could practice her public speaking in front of them. Besides, it had become increasingly clear as our sessions progressed that her fear of public speaking was really just a manifestation of a larger issue: the social anxiety that virtually all adolescents must contend with to one degree or another. For an imaginative girl like Alysia, the perceived threat of social failure was all too easy to visualize. In her words, "I'll never have any friends. Nobody will ever like me. I'm worthless."

To address her social anxiety, I guided Alysia through a series of role-playing exercises and began videotaping her at random intervals to trigger her stress response. Whenever she noticed her muscles tensing up, she was to stop briefly, apply self-regulation, and then continue talking. When she resumed, she could discuss any topic she wished as long as she looked into the camera and spoke in complete sentences. In this way, Alysia learned to speak extemporaneously while controlling her stress response. I erased these video recordings at the end of each session.

Practicing these same skills at home and at school, Alysia began to feel less anxious and more confident. She did, however, continue cutting. The true test of Alysia's burgeoning self-regulation skills came several weeks later when she was assigned to read a paper in English class. I found it hard to believe that the smiling girl who came bouncing into my office the following week was the same girl who had been so sullen and withdrawn a mere two months before. "I'm so excited," she told me. "I did it! I actually did it! I didn't cut! I gave that stupid report in front of everybody and I even messed up a few times. But I didn't cut today!"

It was a lovely moment. Alysia told me that she no longer dreaded going to school and felt much more comfortable with herself and her classmates. She was starting to make new friends and planned to join the school's creative writing club. To her parent's relief and joy, the bloody tissues and T-shirt did not make a reappearance. Alysia had learned better ways to manage her stress. She had stopped cutting for good.

Alysia's Tools for Hope

- **Vision:** I am living in Paris and writing my second novel.
- **Mission Statement:** To write books that open up new worlds for people.
- **Code of Honor:** I'm creative and passionate in every aspect of my life.
- **Perceived Threat(s):**
    1. Other students will laugh and make fun of me. They'll see me as a loser.

2. I'll never have any friends. Nobody will ever like me. I'm worthless.

- **Trigger(s):** Speaking in front of a group of people, especially other students.
- **Intentional Behavior(s):**
  1. Visualizing myself speaking with poise and confidence.
  2. Remaining calm by using my self-regulation skills to keep my body relaxed.
  3. Sharing my creativity with others.

Clyde's Journey

"Clyde" is a 36-year-old army veteran from Richmond, Virginia, whom I first met in August 2012. Clyde had been so deeply affected by the 9/11 tragedy that he was moved to enlist in the army on the day following the attacks. He spent the next four years as an Army Ranger. Clyde's tour of duty included multiple deployments in both Afghanistan and Iraq, where he served with distinction, eventually earning the rank of second lieutenant. In 2005, during his final mission in Afghanistan, Clyde was seriously wounded by a roadside IED (improvised explosive device) that also took the lives of three of his closest friends in his Ranger unit. Traumatized by this experience, Clyde decided not to continue his military career and to return to civilian life once his physical wounds had healed. He received his honorable discharge a few months later.

When he returned home, however, Clyde was beset by terrifying nightmares and flashbacks that made his transition back to civilian life a difficult one. Unable to concentrate for long periods, he dropped out of college twice. Feeling that he was now "too old" to pursue a more satisfying career, he gave up on his dream of becoming a police officer. After five years of mounting desperation, Clyde finally sought PTSD treatment at a nearby Department of Veterans Affairs facility. There, his therapist helped him alleviate some of the worst of his symptoms, including the nightmares that robbed him of restful sleep and the flashbacks that made him distrust himself and question his sanity. However, his civilian life remained a disappointment to him and he often felt restless and unfulfilled.

More recently, Clyde had been struggling with mounting feelings of anxiety and aggression that left him feeling ashamed and depleted. He started spending long hours alone in front of the television, overeating and isolating himself from his former army buddies. He could no longer tolerate any programs or movies that reminded him of the sights and sounds of combat.

His downward spiral reached its nadir one evening during an argument with "Diana," his live-in girlfriend of the past three years. In the midst of this argument, Clyde suddenly snapped, pinning Diana roughly against the wall and threatening to "punch her lights out." Shaken but unhurt, she called the police. Although Diana ultimately declined to press charges, she did level an ultimatum: Clyde must see a therapist or their relationship was over. Clyde agreed, feeling deeply ashamed of his behavior, which he viewed as an unforgiveable breach of his honor and integrity.

Clyde and I began by discussing the emotional problems he was experiencing and how bewildered he felt at his inability to get his life back on track since returning home. "I'm stuck," he told me. "I can't seem to get off the dime." He also expressed considerable skepticism when I explained the Forward-Facing Trauma Therapy process. However, his attitude eased a bit when I described the peripheral vision technique as an option for practicing self-regulation. Clyde already knew the technique well from his marksman training in Ranger School, where it had enabled him to rapidly improve his shooting accuracy.

At the end of the session, I lent Clyde my copy of the book *On Combat*, by Lt. Col. David Grossman, which provides an in-depth analysis of the combat experience and its physiological and psychological effects on soldiers. There, he found additional support for the methods we employ in FFTT, which enabled him to fully invest in our subsequent work together.

Clyde's military training had instilled in him a sense of order and discipline that proved to be highly beneficial to his work with Forward-Facing Trauma Therapy. He approached every homework assignment as if it were a combat mission, with every step carefully planned and executed with precision. Before long, Clyde had completed all of his worksheets and had his "marching orders."

Clyde was afraid that he might act out when triggered or, worse, that he might experience a flashback like the terrifying ones he had endured prior to his first bout of PTSD treatment. So he asked me if he could bring videos of several war scenes he found particularly disturbing to my office so we could watch them together. In this way, I would be able to remind him to stay present and use his new self-regulation skills as soon as he started feeling triggered. I readily agreed and we spent several sessions this way.

Clyde decided that his first intentional behavior would be to switch off the video or leave the room temporarily if his efforts at self-regulation began to fail. We proceeded in this manner until Clyde felt confident enough to pursue his next intentional goal, to tolerate his triggers and maintain his composure without avoidance. Soon, he mastered this too and felt ready to practice at home. Another success ensued, giving him the confidence to begin utilizing FFTT whenever he began to feel anxious or enraged.

Clyde's innate strength and determination were truly remarkable. In only 11 sessions, the fearful, angry man I had met three months before had been transformed. Now that he no longer worried about losing control, he became more confident and relaxed with others. He resumed his workout regimen and let family members and old friends back into his life. Diana noticed the positive changes in his demeanor, self-awareness, and emotional availability, and their relationship began to flourish. In our final session, Clyde said he felt ready to move on with his life and pursue his dream to work in law enforcement. A few months later, he applied for a position with the Virginia State Police and was accepted. At long last, the battle was over. Clyde had finally come home.

Clyde's Tools for Hope

- **Vision:** I'm receiving a commendation for my performance as a police detective.
- **Mission Statement:** I'm a man of honor. I'm here to protect and serve.
- **Code of Honor:** I'm responsible and approach all circumstances from a place of strength and courage.

- **Perceived Threat(s):** I'm going to die.
- **Trigger(s):** Movies and television shows depicting scenes of war.
- **Intentional Behavior(s):**
  1. Leaving the room or changing the channel when I get triggered.
  2. Using my self-regulation skills to maintain my composure without avoidance.

CHAPTER 8

Your New Life Awaits

"Life is never made unbearable by circumstances, but only by lack of meaning and purpose."

— VIKTOR E. FRANKL —

I began this book by quoting the first few lines of Charles Dickens' *A Tale of Two Cities* and observing that we find ourselves at a strange and somewhat paradoxical moment in human history. As I write this last chapter, millions of refugees have fled their homes to escape the seemingly intractable conflicts erupting in an increasingly destabilized Middle East. Here in the United States, the once-cordial debate about our nation's core values has devolved into a mudslinging contest that divides and diminishes us while leaving us ill-prepared to deal with the very real social, economic, and ecological challenges that will shape our future for generations to come.

Yet despite the drumbeat of calamities that so often dominates our media, the human species is far better off today than at any other point in our history. Virtually every objective measure of war, oppression, crime, and violence against women and children has declined sharply during the past hundred years. This durable trend has been exhaustively documented in psychologist Steven Pinker's remarkable book *The Better Angels of Our Nature*.

When we hear about the latest atrocity or threat du jour, humanity's march of progress may seem to have stalled or even reversed. In truth, however, our species is slowly and steadily emerging from its primordial focus on brute survival to one that is much more enlightened and, I daresay, humanistic. In one of his letters, Albert Einstein is said to have written that our sense of separation from one another is a delusion and that our goal must be to widen "our circle of compassion to embrace all living creatures…" Although "(n)obody is able to achieve this completely,…the striving for such achievement is in itself a part of the liberation and a foundation for inner security."[15]

I firmly believe that all of us can achieve this sense of inner security by learning to master and modulate our primitive threat-response systems. When we face the vicissitudes of life with a calm mind and a relaxed body, we change in ways that are deeply satisfying and spiritually profound. As we emerge from confusion into clarity, the delusions and breaches of integrity that have bedeviled us for so long begin to melt away. We feel newly energized and empowered to express our true selves and to connect with others in ways that are more meaningful and loving than ever before. In every facet of our lives, the broken places inside us are healed and we are restored to a path of growth and maturation.

A Note to Clinicians

As a clinical methodology, Forward-Facing Trauma Therapy is well suited to a healthcare system in which managed care providers seek to minimize costs by limiting the number of covered sessions and emphasizing interventions that primarily focus on achieving short-term therapeutic goals. FFTT clients do often achieve miraculous-seeming results with uncommon speed. What's more, with sufficient training, social workers, psychiatric nurses, and paraprofessionals can also learn to employ FFTT effectively, expanding its reach to those who might not otherwise be able to afford therapy.

But Forward-Facing Trauma Therapy is much more than a therapeutic model. Its principles and practices can also be applied productively by teachers with their students, by pastors with their congregants, and in many other non-clinical settings. The widening circle of compassion that FFTT makes possible can spread far beyond our own borders too. As a biologically based methodology for treating stress and trauma, Forward-Facing Trauma Therapy transcends culture and ideology. It is universal in scope, offering hope and healing to every member of the human family.

Parting Thoughts

You and I have come to the end of our journey together. I'd like to thank you for traveling with me and for being such a courageous companion. I hope that you are feeling equal parts challenged and supported after reading this book. I'd also like to leave you with a gift in the form of a solemn promise: If you take the lessons of this book to heart and, in the parlance of 12-step fellowships, "work the steps," you will experience new hope and inspiration. You will feel lighter and more fully yourself. And, one fine morning, you may awaken to find that you have achieved something remarkable that may have previously seemed utterly inconceivable. The stress and fear that once plagued you have been replaced by a sense of comfort and well-being and your future shines with the expectation of many good things coming your way. You have set yourself free.

Notes

1. Pinker, S. (2011). *The better angels of our nature: Why violence has declined.* New York: Viking.
2. National Center for Posttraumatic Stress Disorder. (2015). How common is PTSD? Retrieved from http://www.ptsd.va.gov/public/PTSD-overview/basics/how-common-is-ptsd.asp
3. Van der Kolk, B. Personal communication.
4. National Center for Posttraumatic Stress Disorder. (2015). What is Exposure Therapy? Retrieved from http://www.ptsd.va.gov/public/treatment/therapy-med/treatment-ptsd.asp
5. Ironson, G., Freund, B., Strauss, J., & Williams, J. (2002). Comparison of two treatments for traumatic stress: A community-based study of EMDR and Prolonged Exposure Therapy. *Journal of Clinical Psychology*, 58(1), 113–128.
6. National Center for Posttraumatic Stress Disorder. (2015). PTSD and the military. Retrieved from http://www.ptsd.va.gov/public/PTSD-overview/basics/how-common-is-ptsd.asp
7. Van der Hart, O., & Brown, P. (1992). Abreaction re-evaluated. *Dissociation*, *5*(3), 127–140.

8. American Psychological Association. (2016). Trauma. Retrieved from http://www.apa.org/topics/trauma/
9. Centers for Disease Control and Prevention. (2014). Injury prevention & control: Division of Violence Prevention. Retrieved from http://www.cdc.gov/violenceprevention/acestudy/
10. Rodriguez, T. (2015). Descendants of Holocaust survivors have altered stress hormones. *Scientific American Mind, 26*(2), 10.
11. As cited in Ivey, A. E., Ivey, M. B., & Zalaquett, C. P. (2014). Influencing Skills: Five Strategies for Change. *Intentional Interviewing and Counseling: Facilitating Client Development in a Multicultural Society* (8th ed., p. 348). Belmont, CA: Brooks/Cole CENGAGE Learning.
12. Wolpe, J. (1969). *The practice of behavior therapy.* New York: Pergamon Press.
13. Peterson, J., Freedenthal, S., Sheldon, C., & Anderson, R. (2008). Nonsuicidal self-injury in adolescents. *Psychiatry, 5*(11), 20–26.
14. Cutting Statistics and Self-Injury Treatment. (2015). How widespread is cutting? Retrieved from http://www.teenhelp.com/teen-health/cutting-stats-treatment.html
15. Einstein, A. (1950). As cited in *The New York Times* (29 March 1972) and *New York Post* (28 November 1972).

About the Author

J. Eric Gentry, PhD, LMHC, is a board-certified expert and internationally recognized leader in the field of clinical and disaster traumatology. Since opening his clinical practice in 1990, Dr. Gentry has trained tens of thousands of professionals and paraprofessionals worldwide in the treatment of traumatic stress.

Dr. Gentry received his doctorate from Florida State University, where he studied with Professor Charles Figley, one of the pioneers in the field of traumatic stress. He went on to become one of the founding faculty members and curriculum designers of the Traumatology Institute at Florida State University and later served as co-director of the International Traumatology Institute at the University of South Florida.

Dr. Gentry is the co-author and co-owner of the Traumatology Institute Training Curriculum, which encompasses 17 courses in field and clinical traumatology leading to seven separate certifications. He is also the co-author of the critically acclaimed *Trauma Practice: Tools for Stabilization and Recovery* (third edition), published by Hogrefe & Huber in 2014.

Recognizing the risks of burnout for counseling professionals who work with trauma survivors, Dr. Gentry co-developed the Accelerated Recovery Program (ARP), the world's only evidence-based treatment protocol for compassion fatigue. He is currently a founding board member and vice president of the International Association of Trauma Professionals (IATP) and the owner of Compassion Unlimited, a private psychotherapy, training, and consulting practice based in Sarasota, Florida.

In his career as clinician, researcher, author, and consultant, Dr. Gentry draws equally from the latest research in brain science and his 33 years of clinical experience with trauma survivors. In his spare time, he is an avid hiker, motorcyclist, sportsman, and musician.

Further Information

General information about trauma and its treatment

National Child Traumatic Stress Network (NCTSN): www.nctsnet.org
American Psychological Association: www.apa.org/topics/trauma
Gift from Within PTSD Resources for Survivors and Caregivers: www.giftfromwithin.org
HelpPRO Therapist Finder: www.helppro.com

Government resources

National Center for PTSD: http://www.ptsd.va.gov
Substance Abuse and Mental Health Services Administration: www.samhsa.gov
National Institutes of Mental Health: www.nimh.nih.gov/health/topics/post-traumatic-stress-disorder-ptsd/index.shtml

Professional organizations focused on general trauma research and dissemination

International Society for Traumatic Stress Studies: www.istss.com
European Society for Traumatic Stress Studies: www.estss.org

International Society for the Study of Trauma and Dissociation (ISSTD): www.isst-d.org

Professional training for trauma clinicians

International Association of Trauma Professionals (IATP): www.traumapro.net
Compassion Unlimited: www.CompassionUnlimited.com
Traumatology Institute (Dr. Anna Baranowsky): www.psychink.com
PESI Mental Health Continuing Education: www.pesi.com
Arizona Trauma Institute (Dr. Robert Rhoton): www.aztrauma.org

Information on particular treatment methods

Forward-Facing Trauma Therapy: www.forward-facing.com; www.FFTTbook.com
The EMDR International Association (EMDRIA): www.emdria.org
Sensorimotor Institute: http://www.sensorimotorpsychotherapy.org/home/index.html
National Association of Cognitive-Behavioral Therapists: www.nacbt.org
Neurosequential Model of Therapeutics (Dr. Bruce Perry): www.childtrauma.org
Somatic Experiencing (Dr. Peter Levine): www.traumahealing.org
Intensive Trauma Therapy (Drs. Louis Tinnin & Linda Gantt): www.traumatherapu.us